Published by Pelican Publishing Company, Inc.:
    Bayou Cook Book
    Oaklawn Manor

BAYOU COOK BOOK

Thomas J. Holmes, jr.

Lettering and Sketches
by the Author

with a new section by
Lucile Barbour Holmes

Pelican Publishing Company
Gretna 1990

Manufactured in the United States of America
Published by Pelican Publishing Company, Inc.
1101 Monroe Street, Gretna, Louisiana 70053

We are bringing you these useful, specially selected, recipes of Creole, Bayou, Cooking for your personal pleasure. Most of these recipes have been prepared in our home. Enjoy the seasonings which impart the distinct, not strong, local flavor. They bring forth more taste in the food.

This cook book is in appreciation of the delicious meals that for many years have been planned for me by my wife, Lucile Barbour Holmes. Also, it is dedicated to our five Granddaughters, each of whom is learning and practicing the art of preparing food tastefully.

Thomas J. Holmes, jr.

We gratefully acknowledge permission
to use the following:
Mr. Jay Burnett, for "Herbs and Spices" appearing
in his "Mister Kitchen" column of the "Daily Iberian."
Mr. and Mrs. S. L. Wright, II, for some fine Rice
recipes published in "Poor Man's Rice Cook Book,"
by Wright Laboratory.

Edited by: Joan W. Holmes

CONTENTS

note :   Many new recipes are NOT located
under the descriptive "CONTENTS"
headings.
Let the INDEX be your guide.

PREFACE

This new edition of Bayou Cook Book is larger and has more new and traditional recipes. The all new Index is cross-referenced to make it much easier to find what you want.

An entirely new section, "For the Bride", has been prepared by Lucie Holmes, an active member of our publishing business. And now that we have married granddaughters, she often thinks of her own start years ago. I'm sure most young Brides, and "older Brides" too, will find much of interest here, so look through pages 127 to 147.

The acceptance of Bayou Cook Book has been a most gratifying personal experience. And it is an added pleasure that our family wants it to go on and on.

4

the gentleman's companion

Bayou Cooking

This cook book is called "Bayou Cooking" because nearly all the development of Southern Louisiana was along the Bayou banks. "Creole Cooking," the accepted term, had its origin with the settlers in the early 1700's when the French established the first settlement along the lower Mississippi River. The Creoles. (Webster: "a white descended from the French or Spanish settlers of Louisiana"), not only combined foods and cooking methods of both countries, European and Latin, but soon were introduced to the foods of the Indians, many becoming a part of their cooking and eating habits. Since many of the negro slaves became cooks in the plantation homes, again new cooking ways were added.

Basically our local, Sugar Cane Country cooking is a delightful, tasty, mingling of the ingredients and cooking methods of the French, Spanish, Negro and Indian races. So called "American Cooking", found over most of our country, developed almost entirely from the newcomer's European native homeland. Creole cooking has made an outstanding contribution to our "American Cooking." This is the skillful use of spices, herbs and seasonings, blended to enhance, not overpower, the interesting foods.

Seasoning: "to render palatable by adding salt, pepper, spice, or the like; hence to make more pungent, piquant, etc.," (Webster).

Mr. Jay Burnett, a resident of a nearby town on the banks of Bayou Tech, Louisiana, has a column titled "Mister Kitchen" in the local daily paper. He has most kindly given permission for the use of the following clear discussion of seasonings. Again, my thanks.

"A lot of pseudo cooks know the difference between an herb and a verb but very, very few of them know when an herb is a herb and not a spice. There's a tendency to lump herbs and spices into one category and call 'em under one name: Spices. And that's where a lot of cooking mistakes become bigger mistakes.

"Spices are parts of plants from the tropics... the bark, leaves, seeds, shells and other aromatic parts that are suitable for seasoning or preserving.

"Herbs are leaves of temperate zone plants, such as dill, marjoram, oregano, savory, thyme, sage and mint. (The last named growing outside the writers door. t.j.h.)

"You can't achieve proper results in the use of herbs in home food preparation thinking that if a little is good a lot is even better. Herbs must be used with caution and it's better to use too little than to 'slug' the dish with a flavor your family probably won't like. So, let's take an easy lesson.

"<u>Bouquet Garni</u>. Many recipes call for "bouquet garni," which means that a combination of herbs should appear in the finished dish. I suggest that you tie the herbs in a small cheesecloth bag and cook in your soup or stew until you get the desired strength or flavor. For a real good garni try mixing equal parts (about ½ tsp. of each) of basil, thyme, marjoram and savory. As you progress with your learning which herb gives what flavor, you can lower or raise the amounts for better taste balance.

"<u>Fines Garni</u>. This means finely chopped herbs which are added directly to the dish under preparation. This scatters the herbs throughout the completed dish and is recommended for roast meats, chopped meats, ground meats, omelets, sauces, as pies and salads. In cooking salt and pepper are to be considered as separate integral entities to most dishes, thus they are classed as prime flavor-makers, much the same as a woman's base coat of face make-up is the primer for bringing out her best features. In addition to salt and pepper there are seven basics which I've found helpful in bringing out flavor in certain dishes. You may file this away for future reference; it will save you a lot of time in deciding just what herb or spice makes what dish taste tastier.

"Basil: A first class partner for tomatoes. The leaves and tender stems of basil plants are always part of Italian tomato paste. This herb is also good in vegetable soups and gives tomato juice cocktail a real lip-smacking touch.

"Bay Leaves: One bay leaf or even a half will flavor a whole casserole. You'll also find bay leaves add a special zing to fish chowders, seafood gumbos and to tomato soup.

"Dill: Fresh dill is a dainty, lacy herb that's wonderful when chopped and added to salads. You're doubtless familiar with the dill used in pickling but give a try to dill seed sprinkled on potato salad, macaroni, or in sauerkraut. You'll be nicely surprised, as will your family. Might as well give them something different in the way of flavor.

"Marjoram: This is a member of the mint family. It adds freshness to meats, fruits or to vegetables. Sprinkle it over lamb while it's cooking. Another idea: cook it with lima beans for extra flavor. Also, give it a light try in the stuffing for the chicken, ravioli, chopped meat or breaded cutlets. I like a little of it to boost the flavor of lima beans, peas, or all kinds of string beans.

<u>"Mint</u>: Most imbibers associate mint with a drink called "mint julep," but has a lot more uses as a flavoring. Try it in fruit cups, stewed fruits, green peas, glazed peas and carrots, boiled new potatoes and especially lamb roast.

<u>"Rosemary</u>: This fresh, sweet herb looks like a pine needle but there the similarity stops. Use it sparingly in soups, stews and lamb dishes. You'll also find it gives added zest in dressing for duck, chicken, turkey and pork.

<u>"Thyme</u>: The leaves of fresh thyme are tender as are the stems. Both are strongly aromatic and are to be used sparingly. Add to meat loaves, chowders, stews and in stuffing for poultry. Thyme adds a special flavor to aspics, vegetable juice cocktails, peas, carrots, onions and pickled beets.

"As you progress with your use of herbs and spices, you'll find a new world of flavor in your dishes. But start slowly and learn as you go. By all means don't overdo the use of any herb or spice. You can put in too much, but you can't take it out."

(author: many herb/spice charts are available; get one and keep in your kitchen)

Common Seasonings for use with various foods. This is a way you can vary a given recipe by trying an alternate seasoning when indicated.

for Aspics: use _Basil_ for tomato aspic and ×_Thyme_ for all aspics.

for Beverages: use _Basil_ for tomato juice cocktails; _Mint_ for tea and juleps; ×_Thyme_ with vegetable juice cocktails

for Fowl: use Marjoram for poultry stuffing; ×_Rosemary_ for chicken, duck and turkey dressings; ×_Thyme_ with same fowl dressings.

for Fruit: use _Marjoram_ to add freshness; _Mint_ with fruit cups and stewed fruit.

for Meat: use _Bay Leaves_ with casseroles; Marjoram with chopped meat and breaded cutlets, also lamb; _Mint_ with lamb roast; ×_Rosemary_ with stews, lamb or pork; ×_Thyme_ with meat loaves and stews.

for Vegetables: use _Basil_ with tomatoes; _Dill_ with macaroni and sauerkraut; _Marjoram_ with lima beans, peas and string beans; _Mint_ with carrots, green peas and boiled new potatoes; ×_Thyme_ with peas, carrots, onions or pickled beets.

for Salads: use _Dill_ seed for potato salad.

for Soups: use _Basil_ with vegetables; _Bay Leaves_ with tomato, fish chowder and seafood gumbo; ×_Rosemary_ with soups; ×_Thyme_ with chowders.

Note: ×please use these herbs sparingly!

THE seafoods of Louisiana, a product of our coastal waterways, miles of coastal swamps and bays and the bountiful Gulf of Mexico, have been used since the beginning of recorded history. Today our frozen seafoods are shipped nation-wide, especially our oysters and shrimp.

THUS we start our recipes with good seafood dishes. Shrimp having so many uses we like to keep both raw and cleaned shrimp on hand. The raw shrimp, headless, are placed immediately in containers, covered with water and frozen. Several pounds are cleaned and deveined. (There is a very fine kitchen "tool" available to make this process quite simple.) The clean (sometimes called "green") shrimp are then boiled in seasoned water. Some are frozen in their own water while the remainder are then stored in the refrigerator section covered with liquid. Thus we try to have on hand prepared shrimp for instant use in gumbos, cocktails, salads or hot dishes. Now, "à la bonne cuisine", y'all......

des crevettes

des poisson

des tortues

des crabes

frogga

des ecrivesses

Shrimp (des crevetts)   Crabs (des crabes)   Fish (des poissons)
Oysters (des huitres)

Shrimp Newberg Teche

2 tbsp. butter   dash pepper
3 tbsp. flour   1/8 tsp. paprika
2 cups light cream   1/4 cup cooking sherry
1/4 tsp. salt   4-6 slices buttered toast

2 cups cleaned, cooked, shrimp, cut in
large pieces. (1 pound before boiled)
Melt butter in top of double boiler. Add
flour, stir well. Pour cream in all at once;
immediately stir over moderate heat.
Continue to cook until thickened, stirring
constantly. Season with salt, pepper and
paprika. Add the sherry, a little at a
time, stirring well. Add shrimp, cook,
until heated through.
Serve on triangles of toast, or place
in chaffing dish and let guests
spoon Newberg on to toast.
4 to 6 servings.

Shrimp Remoulade

4 tbsp. olive oil (do not substitute)
2 tbsp. wine vinegar
1 tsp. salt (less if desired)
3 tsp. Creole mustard. (or use a
        mustard containing horse-radish).
Few drops tobasco (or any pepper sauce).
dash paprika
few sprigs parsley, minced
6 shallots, minced
2 stalks celery, minced
Mix a French dressing of olive oil,
vinegar and salt. Add the remaining
ingredients and pour over boiled shrimp
placed on torn lettuce leaves. Be sure to
let stand 4 or 5 hours before serving.

Boiled Shrimp

1 quart water	1 bay leaf
1 stalk celery, cut-up	1 tsp. salt
1/2 cup onion, sliced	3 lemon slices,
2 drops pepper sauce	thin
2 pounds raw shrimp	1 clove garlic

Combine water, celery, onion and season-ings in a saucepan and bring to a quick boil. Lower heat and simmer while cleaning shrimp. Shell and clean shrimp and add lemon slices to pot with raw shrimp. Boil slowly until shrimp are pink and done (10 to 15 minutes) stirring occasionally. Let shrimp cool in liquid in pot. Remove shrimp reserving liquor for future use.

Excess shrimp can be frozen in a sealed container covered with own liquor. They can be kept several days in refrigerator covered with liquid.

Shrimp Cocktail sauce
(good with crabmeat)

To 3/4 cup chili sauce, or catsup, add 1 1/2 tbsp. lemon juice, 1 tbsp. worcester sauce, 1 tbsp. horse radish, 2 drops pepper sauce, 1/4 tsp. salt and 1 tsp. grated onion. Mix well and chill thoroughly.

Barbecued Shrimp

Clean raw shrimp, leaving tails on. Boil with seasonings adding 1/2 tsp., or more, of Liquid Smoke for each quart of water. Serve hot or cold for dipping by tails in your favorite barbecue sauce.
Use outdoors or indoors.

Curried Shrimp

1½ cups boiled shrimp
3 onions, medium size
1 ripe tomato
1 tsp. sugar
2 tbsp. curry powder
2 tbsp. celery, cut fine
2 tbsp. butter

Fry onion in butter until soft. Add tomato, celery, sugar, curry powder and enough shrimp liquor (or water) to allow ingredients to simmer for 45 minutes over a slow fire. Add more liquor if it seems to dry out. Now add shrimp and cook 15 minutes longer. Remove from fire and let stand one-half hour for shrimp to absorb seasoning. Serve hot with boiled rice; use Major Grey's Chutney if available.

Shrimp Creole

2 cups boiled shrimp
2 tbsp. melted butter
1 cup onion, chopped
1 cup bell pepper, chopped
½ garlic clove, chopped
1 pint tomatoes
½ tsp. paprika

Melt butter, add paprika and stir till blended. Add onion, bell pepper and garlic. Simmer until tender, then add tomatoes, salt and pepper. Boil 5 minutes. Place shrimp in this mixture and cook slowly 20 minutes. Serve hot over rice. For six servings.

oyster lugger

Shrimp Jambalaya

¼ cup cooking oil
1 large onion, chopped
3 stalks celery, chopped
1 bell pepper, chopped
1 tsp. salt — ¼ tsp. red pepper
1 can tomato sauce
1 pound raw, cleaned, shrimp
3 cups water — (part shrimp liquor, if any)
1½ cups raw rice

Put the onion, celery and bell pepper in a heavy skillet with the oil and cook over a medium heat for 15 minutes - do not brown. Add the salt, red pepper, tomato sauce, liquid and raw shrimp. Cook for 10 minutes over medium heat. Remove from fire, add raw rice and some chopped parsley if desired. Pour in a 2 quart casserole, cover and bake at 350°F. for one hour, or until rice is done. Do not stir or uncover during cooking.

Shrimp-Crab Meat Casserole

1 large eggplant
1 large onion, chopped
1 pound raw shrimp, cleaned
2 tbsp. cooking oil
1 cup bread crumbs
1 cup cooked crab meat

Cut and dice the peeled eggplant and soak in salt water. Cook onions in oil until wilted. Add raw shrimp and continue cooking over medium heat until onions brown slightly. Then add eggplant and cook slowly until very tender. Add most of bread crumbs (moisten these) and mix well. Cook over low heat to dressing consistency. Put in casserole, sprinkle with bread crumbs and bake at 350°F. until lightly browned.

Shrimp à la King

1 can cream of mushroom soup.
½ cup (or less) shrimp liquor or milk
1 tbsp. pimiento, minced
½ tsp. celery salt
  shrimp for 2 servings; if large, cut
      in half.
2 tbsp. cooking sherry (optional)
Put mushroom soup in saucepan and add liquid. Stir over low heat until smooth, then add shrimp, pimiento and celery salt. Cook over medium heat until shrimp are hot, stirring only to mix. If sherry is used, add a few minutes before removing from fire. Serve on buttered toast or in patty shells.
  Along the Bayou this dish is often served in a French loaf of bread, hollowed out, buttered and toasted in oven. This is a quick, tasty dish for two, especially when cooked shrimp are at hand.

Oysters, Pan-Broiled

3 dozen oysters
6 tbsp. butter, level
1 lemon, juice
  parsley, few sprigs, chopped
  few drops pepper sauce, to taste
6 slices toast
Melt butter in saucepan, drop in oysters, add lemon juice, parsley and pepper sauce. Add salt if necessary. Cook a few minutes until edges of oysters curl. Allow 6 oysters to each piece of toast and pour juice over.

Oyster Cocktail Sauce

Mix ⅔ catsup and ⅓ horse-radish (or less), add a few drops of lemon juice, plus a dash of pepper sauce to taste.

OYSTER LOAF

1 unsliced loaf French bread
1 dozen oysters
  bread crumbs or cracker dust
  salt and pepper
1 egg
  cooking oil

Cut off top of French bread, scoop out inside and toast loaf. Butter inside generously and keep warm. Dry oysters in paper towel. Beat egg with salt and pepper, slowly adding a small amount of cream. Dip each oyster in the egg mixture, then place the oyster in the crumbs and thoroughly cover all sides. Fry in shallow oil until brown and drain on absorbent paper. Fill hollow of French loaf with the fried oysters, then replace top and warm in oven.
Provide catsup.
A family favorite along Coastal Louisiana.

SCALLOPED OYSTERS

2/3 cup melted butter (oleo)
3 cups stale bread crumbs (cracker crumbs)
1 tsp. onion, grated
1 tsp. salt
1/8 tsp. pepper
1 1/2 pints oysters
1/3 cup oyster liquor or water
1/3 cup cream

Combine butter, crumbs, onion and seasonings. Drain oysters reserving any liquor. Place a layer of oysters in a greased, shallow baking dish; top with a layer of crumbs and then with remaining oysters. Pour liquid and cream over layers. Top with remaining crumbs and sprinkle with paprika. Bake in a moderate oven (375°F.) 25 to 30 minutes, or until browned.
Serves six.

OYSTERS à la Jay Burnett

24 large oysters on half shell
24 1 inch x 1 inch squares bacon
   Trappey's "Spice Up" table
       seasoning.

Arrange oysters on broiler pan,
sprinkle lightly with Spice-Up.
Place square of bacon on each
oyster, shove under broiler
flame 8 inches. When the bacon
is crisp the oysters are ready
for eating.

Jay adds: When the oysters are
placed under the broiler start
smacking your lips. The liquid
remaining after the oyster is
removed is mighty good, too, so
don't discard it.

The recipe will serve 6 oysters per
person but you can bet more will
be requested.

OYSTERS JAMBALAYA

12 (or more!) oysters
1 tbsp. shortening
1 tbsp. flour
1 onion, minced
1 cup boiling water
1 cup hot oyster water
  salt, cayenne pepper, minced
    parsley

Lightly brown flour in shortening
and add onion. When well
browned pour in boiling water,
stir, and let cook thick. Now add
hot oyster water and season
well with all seasonings. (A drop
or two of pepper sauce can be
used if desired.) When well
blended put in oysters and let
simmer a few minutes. Add enough
boiled rice to absorb liquid and stir
well until done. This is a simple yet

extremely palatable dish and makes a meal, served with hot bread and plenty butter.

Oysters Rockefeller

A bit 'fancy' - but so good!
6 oysters for each serving
¼ pound butter, melted
1 small bunch parsley
1 small bunch spinach
½ stalk celery
1 bunch green onion tops
1 small bunch beet tops
  juice of one or two lemons

Put out pie plates and fill each with coarse (ice cream) salt. Place six oysters on half shell in each plate. Grind all of the greens and the celery very fine, add melted butter and lemon juice. Now put a teaspoon of this on each oyster, place pie plates in broiler and cook rapidly until the oysters curl. Serve in plates in which cooked. (Protect table from the very hot plates).

Oyster Stuffing

1½ cups butter or oleo
½ cup onion, finely chopped
1 qt. oysters
½ cup celery, chopped
2½ to 3½ qts. stale bread and stale
        corn bread, half and half
1 tbsp. salt
¼ tsp. pepper
1½ tsps. Poultry seasoning.

Heat butter in large, heavy, skillet, add onion, chopped oysters and celery. Cook until onion soft, not brown. Add bread and corn bread cubes and seasonings. Heat until bread cubes are lightly browned and butter is absorbed, stirring constantly.

This makes a dry, crumbly, stuffing. If you prefer a moist stuffing, add milk to desired state.
This recipe for a 12 to 16 pound Turkey.

SEAFOOD GUMBO

"Gumbo" is such a truly Southern Louisiana dish the following recipe is given in detail and admonishes those preparing this dish to take "time a plenty" during the cooking process. The unique gumbo flavor results from slow cooking, beginning with the browning of the roux to a deep golden brown and on to the final cooking. This slow, careful, attention alone blends all of the ingredients resulting in the true "Gumbo" taste.

1 pound raw shrimp, cleaned	1 large onion, diced	salt and pepper to taste
½ pound cooked crabmeat	¼ cup bell pepper, diced	liquid as needed. (Water,
2 cups oysters	½ cup celery, diced	or replace some water with
1 heap. tbsp. crisco + 1½ tbsp. flour	1 bay leaf	shrimp liquor or chicken broth)

Make the roux by heating, in a heavy pot, enough oil to cover bottom well. Add flour, stirring, until absorbed with oil. At a low heat stir continually until flour is a fairly dark brown. Burnt flour ruins any roux—and the Gumbo. Add onions, celery and bell pepper to the roux, cooking over low heat, stirring until the onions are wilted, not brown. Add sufficient liquid to make number of servings desired. (For the ingredients listed, about 2 quarts boiling water.) Put the raw, cleaned, shrimp in the pot, add the bay leaf, and simmer for one hour, stirring now and then. Add the crab meat and oysters about 15 minutes before serving. Serve in a soup tureen with a large bowl of steamed rice, or in soup plates place a mound of rice and ladle in the Gumbo. A pinch of filé may be put in each serving, or placed on table for individual desires. A good main dish with salad, garlic bread.

Oyster Soup *family recipe*

Place ½ stick butter (oleo) into a 2 qt. sauce pan and ½ cup chopped shallots. Sauté until onion is wilted, then add 2 cups oysters and cook until oysters curl. Meanwhile, melt 2 tbsp. butter in a medium sauce pan, add one tbsp. flour and blend. Add one chopped shallot, cook two minutes, then gradually add two cups milk. (Or evaporated milk with ½ water). Now add salt and pepper to taste. Stir and let come to scalding point. Pour mixture <u>into</u> the pan of hot oysters, stir gently and serve with saltine crackers.

Shrimp Bisque

2 pounds cleaned, boiled, shrimp
3 slices stale bread
1 can condensed tomato soup
1 bay leaf
½ onion, chopped
   minced parsley
   salt and pepper to taste
   cooking oil

Cut shrimp in half. Soak bread in water just to soften and season highly with the bay leaf, onion, parsley, salt and pepper. Put in the sauce pan, with a small amount of oil, and cook, stirring to achieve a dressing (fowl) consistency. When well blended, add the tomato soup and an equal quantity of water. Now add the cooked shrimp. If too thick add water sparingly. Shrimp liquor may be used for part of water.

BOILED CRABS

12 large crabs
1 garlic clove, minced
1 large onion, chopped
2 tsp. salt
2 bay leaves, whole
2 stalks celery, chopped
1 lemon, sliced thin
  pepper sauce to taste
Put about 3 quarts of water to boil in a heavy pot. Prepare seasonings and add to boiling water for about six minutes. Now add live crabs and boil for about 15 minutes; test by pulling off a claw with tongs. Let crabs cool in the pot. Serve informally whole or remove meat for use as you desire.

CRAB IMPERIAL

2 lbs. crab meat, claw
2 tsp. chopped pimiento
2 tsp. whole capers
1 tsp. worcester sauce
6 drops pepper sauce
1 tsp. salt
½ cup mayonnaise
Blend seasonings into mayonnaise, pour over the crab meat and toss together lightly. Place the crab meat on scallop shells and top off with an additional tablespoon of mayonnaise. Sprinkle with paprika and bake for twenty minutes at 375°F. Serve at once. Serves six.

friendly aside : be confident in your cooking ← but _please_ follow your recipes implicitly.

Why not profit by the other fellow's mistake? (could be, mistakes)

Stuffed Crabs

2 cups crab meat, cooked
2 tbsp. onions, minced
¼ pound butter, or oleo
½ cup dried bread crumbs, rolled
¼ cup water
½ lemon, juice
1 tbsp. parsley, minced
2 hard-boiled eggs, finely chopped
   extra bread crumbs, fine

Brown onion in butter, add crab meat, ½ cup bread crumbs, water and lemon juice. Cook from 15 to 20 minutes. Add parsley, hard-boiled eggs and put into shells or a baking dish. Sprinkle with bread crumbs and put in oven a few minutes before serving to heat and brown crumbs. This will make about eight servings.

Baked Crab Meat

1 stalk celery   1 tbsp. flour
½ bell pepper   2 tbsp. sherry
1 stick butter or oleo – bread crumbs
2 cups crab meat   1 pint milk

Chop celery and green (bell) pepper very fine. Put butter in deep skillet and add the celery and pepper and then the crab meat. Next, stir in smoothly the milk and flour. Cook until the mixture is creamy, then add sherry. Put into a baking dish, cover with bread crumbs, dot with butter and bake at 350°F. until crumbs are brown.

IDLEWILD CRAB CHOPS

1 lb. crabmeat, fresh or frozen   1 cup bread crumbs   1 onion, grated
8 tbsp. butter or oleo   2 eggs   2 cups milk
                              8 tbsp. flour

(The following is as given to me:) — "When the moon is full and crabs
                        are _fat_, catch several dozen and
boil 20 minutes in hot water seasoned with "Crab Boil Seasoning," lemon
slices, pepper and salt. Let cool in pot, remove, clean and pick out the
white meat, the fat if you like it, and the claw (dark) meat, being careful
to remove all shell pieces. While the crabs are boiling make a thick white
sauce by melting butter (oleo) adding flour and onion and blending well.
Add milk slowly and cook, stirring constantly, until very thick and
smooth. Mix with crabmeat and bread crumbs. Shape into chops or
patties and chill for several hours until firm. Then dip in bread crumbs
again. These freeze well, stacked in a pan with a layer of foil or
doubled wax paper between to separate easily, and tightly sealed in a
plastic freezer bag. When ready to serve (without defrosting) place
chops on a buttered toast pan with a dab of butter on top of each.
Heat in a hot oven until lightly browned, about 10 minutes".

                              Lurline and Edith
                              -and they _do_ catch
                                their own crabs!

Crawfish (des écrevisses)

Crawfish have been, for many years, a spring delicacy from our Bayou waters. Now, with crawfish "farms" being developed, they are available outside.

Crawfish Etouffee

4 pounds fresh crawfish	3 tbsp. shallot tops, minced	¼ tsp. corn starch
3 onions, finely chopped	3 tbsp. parsley, minced	¼ cup cold water
¼ cup celery, chopped	½ tsp. tomato paste	salt and pepper
cooking oil		dash of pepper sauce

Boil crawfish, remove from fire and peel tails. Cover saucepan bottom lightly with oil, heat and add onions, celery and tomato paste. Cook over medium heat until onions are wilted. Add crawfish tails. Dissolve corn starch in cold water, add to pan, stirring constantly. Season to taste with salt and pepper and pepper sauce, if desired. Bring to a boil in uncovered pan over medium heat and cook for 15 minutes. Add onion tops and parsley, mix well and serve with steamed rice. Serves four.

Lagoon Scampi

8 doz. crawfish tails ▪ 1 cup light rum ▪ 4 sticks cinnamon ▪ 1 tbsp. nutmeg ▪ 6 cloves

Sauté crawfish in olive oil. Add spices and steep for 30 minutes. Remove spices and pour heated rum over crawfish. Serve on slices of toasted French bread. Serves four.

CREOLE CRAWFISH

½ cup cooking oil
1 cup flour
1 cup onions, chopped
3 garlic cloves, sliced
2 tbsp. bell pepper, chopped
2 tbsp. onion tops (green) chopped
2 tbsp. parsley, chopped
3 cups cold water
3 cups cleaned crawfish tails

Flour is added to hot oil and stirred well until dark brown. Add onions, garlic and bell pepper. Simmer 10 minutes then add water and crawfish and cook slowly 30 minutes. Add onion tops, parsley, salt and pepper. Serve over hot, boiled, rice. Serves 8.

SPANISH CRAWFISH

½ cup olive oil (do not substitute)
1 bell pepper, sliced
   salt and pepper to taste
1 cup dry Spanish sherry
2 cups cleaned crawfish tails

Roll crawfish in flour and sauté in oil about 5 minutes. Remove crawfish and sauté green pepper in oil for 10 minutes over low flame. Return crawfish to pan and simmer for two minutes. Now add sherry, stir, cover and cook for three minutes over high flame. Serve with broccoli and hot, boiled, rice. Season the broccoli with lemon butter or hollandaise sauce. Serves 6.

28

Catfish Fortnightly ~emmo

6 catfish fillets
2 pts. coffee cream
1½ tbsp. flour
¼ lb. butter
1 cup mushrooms, sautéed
1 lb. crabmeat
1 lb. shrimp, boiled
½ cup cooking sherry

Season fillets with butter, salt
and white pepper. Place in a
lightly buttered 2 qt. casserole and
bake in a 325°F. oven about 20-25
minutes. While fish is baking make
a cream sauce with the butter,
flour and cream, seasoned to taste.
Add crabmeat, mushrooms and shrimp.
Heat over low flame, then add
sherry. Spoon the hot sauce over
the baked fish separating fillets
for sauce penetration. Garnish with
pimiento crosses or green pepper. (6)

Trout Almondine ~herbert

4 filet of trout
milk
salt and pepper
flour
butter (use if possible, in place of oleo)
½ cup slivered almonds

Dip filets in milk, then in seasoned
flour. In skillet, melt butter to cover
bottom fully and fry filets until brown,
turning over as needed. Remove
from pan to a warm platter. Sprinkle
heavily with almonds and pour butter
sauce over all. _Sauce_ : Over low heat
melt ¾ stick of pure butter, add a
pinch of flour, or two, ½ teaspoon
worcester sauce and stir well. Add
lemon juice to taste.

BAYOU COURTBOUILLON

4 to 5 pounds of any firm-fleshed fish.   salt, red and black pepper
4 large onions, chopped   ½ green pepper, chopped
Cooking oil   2 cloves garlic, chopped
1 can tomato sauce

At least an hour before hand season the fish, cut up in chunks, with salt, red and black pepper and let the fish stand. Roll the garlic and green pepper in a mixture of salt and pepper dampened with vinegar. Cut an incision in each piece of fish and place pieces of garlic and green pepper within. Sauté the onion in oil until tender. Add tomato sauce and cook slowly until tomato separates from the oil; now add water slowly to prevent sticking. Add seasoned fish to sauce and cover. Cook over a low fire from 40 to 45 minutes – do *not* stir. Move the pot from side to side to prevent sticking until liquid forms. A true Creole dish. Serve with boiled rice.

Baked Red Fish with Wine Sauce

1 red fish, medium size
4 or 5 thin onion slices
   salt and pepper
1 cup white wine
1 garlic clove, finely chopped
3 tbsp. lemon juice
1 bay leaf
¼ cup melted butter

Wash fish and split open; sprinkle salt and pepper inside and outside and insert onion slices. Put fish together and place in a shallow baking pan or oven-proof platter. Combine wine, garlic, lemon juice, bay leaf and melted butter thoroughly and pour over fish, reserving some for basting and some to serve with the fish. Bake at 400°F. allowing 10 minutes for each pound. Baste occasionally. When done, fish separates with a fork.

Broiled Fish Fillets

French dressing   salt and pepper
lemon juice   3 tbsp. melted butter

Wash fillets and marinate in French dressing an hour before broiling. Dry thoroughly. Place fillets on a well greased broiler pan; sprinkle with salt, pepper and lemon juice, then brush with melted butter. Place two inches from heat. Broil 10 to 15 minutes, or until richly brown. Test with a fork in the thickest part of the fish. When it is done it will flake easily. Baste several times. Serve with lemon butter, or try pressing the juice of a large garlic clove in with the lemon butter — blending well.

TURTLE (turtue)

turtle SAUCE PIQUANT

"peck" fourmy, bayou Teche

-a 7 to 8 lb. turtle; 1½ stalks celery, cut fine; 1 bell pepper, chopped fine; 1 large onion, chopped fine; 8 cloves garlic, chopped fine; 1 cup corn oil; ½ cup all purpose flour; 1 No.1 can tomato sauce; ½ can tomato purée; 1 tbsp. worcester sauce; 1 tsp. paprika; 1½ tsp. seafood seasoning; 2 tbsp. sweet pickle vinegar; salt and pepper to taste; 1 cup cooking sherry wine.

REMOVE turtle meat from shell, cut in pieces about size of a large egg and wash in warm water four times. Cut up celery, garlic, bell pepper and set aside. Put 1 cup corn oil in a thick pot. Heat oil until very hot, add flour, stirring constantly until flour is a light brown color. Add celery, onion, etc., stirring constantly until well mixed. Lower fire and let cook ½ hour, stirring well to keep seasonings from burning or sticking. Now, if roux too thick, add one or two cups hot water and stir for about 3 minutes, cooking slowly. Add tomato sauce and tomato purée, worcester sauce, paprika and seafood seasoning. Add the sweet pickle vinegar and salt and pepper. Let cook slowly for about 3 minutes. Add raw turtle meat to mixture and cook meat in mixture on a medium fire until tender. When tender add sherry wine. Control turtle meat mixture; if too thick add small amounts hot water; if too thin, remove turtle meat, make a mixture of a little corn starch and water. Pour into gravy and cook slowly, then replace meat and heat slowly. Serve with rice.

TURTLE SOUP   from "peck" four.my, bayou teche, louisiana.

1 No. 2 can tomato sauce
4 medium size Irish potatoes, diced
4 green onion stalks cut in small pieces
8 small garlic cloves, cut very fine
½ lemon
¼ lb. butter (oleo)
    salt and pepper to taste
½ cup parsley, cut very fine
2 stems celery, cut fine
1 large bell pepper, cut fine
1 cup white wine
7 to 8 lb. turtle

Remove turtle meat from shell, cut in small pieces or put through meat grinder using coarse or wide open blade. Wash meat about four times in cold water before cutting into small pieces or grinding. Place turtle meat into a four quart very thick pot or kettle. Add 2½ to 3 quarts of cold water. Boil 15 minutes, then skim off all foam. Add all ingredients except potatoes. when soup is almost cooked, add potatoes and let cook until potatoes are cooked. While potatoes are cooking, if the broth has reduced add 1 pint of hot water and let boil to right consistency and until potatoes are done. Remove from fire and add wine. The complete recipe makes approximately 2 qts. of soup.

Some Sherry Wine uses: sherry custard pie; sherry pudding; sherry eggnog; sherry Froth; fruit sauce; jelly. (and another page is filled!)

for your Seafood Recipes

~ notes ~

<u>Symbols Used Herein</u>: *(all measurements are level.)*
1 tsp. = 1 Teaspoon   1 tbsp. = 1 Tablespoon   1 pt. = 1 Pint
1 qt = 1 Quart   1 gal. = 1 Gallon
<u>NOTE</u>: *<u>Worcester</u> used instead of correct <u>Worcestershire</u> to save lettering.*

MEAT DISHES

quelques plates de viande —

Daube Glacé

3 lbs. veal roast	1 tbsp. salt
2 tbsp. shortening	2 bay leaves
6 cups water	3 sprigs parsley
1 onion, chopped	1 tbsp. gelatine
1 cup celery, chopped coarse	(softened in ¼
1 bell pepper, chopped coarse	cup cold water)

Rub salt on roast and sear dark brown in shortening. When nicely browned, pour off all grease, add water and onion, cover tightly and allow to boil slowly. Cook about an hour, then add the celery, bell pepper and bay leaves. Continue cooking until meat is very tender and can be pulled apart with a fork. Add the parsley, minced fine. Remove from fire and add the gelatine. When cooled, pour into mold and chill. This dish is tastier if prepared the day before serving. Unmold and slice with a very sharp knife.

Grillades with Gravy

1 round steak	1 tbsp. shortening
½ can tomatoes	1½ tbsp. flour
1 large onion	1 clove garlic
salt and pepper	½ bell pepper, minced

Cut steak in pieces for individual servings. Fry till brown in hot shortening, then remove and set aside. Brown flour in same pan, add chopped onions and wilt them. Now add tomatoes, bell pepper, garlic and salt and pepper to taste. Put meat back in pan, pour in enough water to cover (beef broth is best if on hand) and cook slowly until meat is tender, about 1½ to 2 hours. (Use meat tenderizer for shorter cooking time)

old time "Spider" fry pan

36

Pork Roast

3 inch slice of pork from pot roast cut
salt and pepper
monsodium glutamate
2 garlic cloves, halved
3 tbsp. shortening
1 can sweet potatoes, drained

With sharp knife make 4 incisions in
meat and place ½ garlic clove in each
cut. Season both sides of roast with
glutamate, salt and pepper. In heavy pot,
with a tight lid, heat shortening and
place meat in, searing both sides. Brown
each side thoroughly, covering pot to
retain steam. Add small amount of
water, cooking over very low fire till
meat is tender; from one to two hours.
Remove lid only to check amount of
gravy. Do not permit to dry. When done,
remove meat, keep warm. Put sweet
potatoes in gravy, cover tightly and
roast until hot. Serve with pork-gravy.

Creole Hamburger

1 pound ground beef
1 egg
1 tbsp. catsup
1 tbsp. Creole er other prepared mustard
½ onion, chopped
3 garlic cloves, minced
¼ cup bread crumbs
salt and pepper to taste

Combine all ingredients and shape
into cakes. Fry till cooked to your
taste. Good served with creamed
potatoes and peas. Note: For some
time we have used NO oil when cooking ground meat. Place a thin layer of
table salt over bottom of pan and
cook hamburgers on this.
Salt layer does not affect taste.

Beef and Rice with Cheese

2 cups raw rice
1 lb. ground beef
¼ cup cooking oil
1 tbsp. chili powder
2 tsp. salt
¼ tsp. garlic powder

1 large onion, chopped
2 cans tomato sauce
3 cups water
1 10-oz. package of
    sharp Cheddar
    cheese, large pieces

Sauté meat and onion in oil for 15 minutes over medium heat, stirring to prevent sticking. Remove from fire and add all of remaining ingredients. Pour in a 2-quart greased casserole. Be sure pieces of cheese are well distributed. Cover tightly and bake for one hour at 400°F. without stirring. Turn oven down and stir mixture lightly <u>once</u>. Cover again and bake 30 more minutes.

Louisiana Meat Loaf

1 pound ground chuck beef ground with
    ½ pound lean pork
1 cup bread crumbs
½ cup red wine
3 tbsp. parsley, minced
3 tbsp. onions, chopped
¼ tsp. pepper

3 tbsp. celery leaves
    finely chopped
1 tsp. salt
¼ tsp. paprika
¼ tsp. garlic salt

Moisten bread crumbs thoroughly with red wine, then mix with all other ingredients into a loaf, kneading with fingers is best. Put in a baking dish and cover with the following sauce: mix together 1 cup tomato catsup, ¼ cup wine vinegar, 2 tbsp. worcester sauce, 2 tbsp. chili powder, 1 tsp. salt and ¼ tsp. pepper sauce. Place dish in a 325°F. oven for 1¼ hours, basting frequently. Do not allow to dry out. Add beef consomme for basting when needed.

38

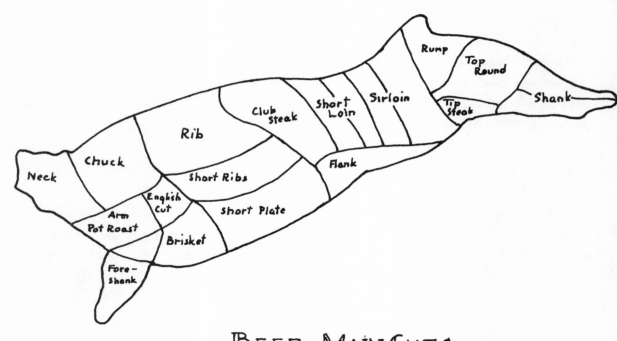

BEEF-MAIN CUTS

Baked Hash

2 pounds brisket — 1 onion — 2 tablespoons butter — 3 potatoes

Use lean brisket remaining from a rich soup. Put the brisket through a meat grinder; chop onions and sauté lightly in butter. Mix with ground meat, season highly with salt and pepper, put in a greased baking dish and cover with potatoes that have been boiled, seasoned and mashed. Dot with butter and bake until potatoes are well browned.

Louisiana Rice Dressing ("dirty rice" locally)

(Included here, since it is so often used with many meats and fowl.)

½ cup cooking oil	¼ tsp. red pepper	2 tsp. salt
½ lb. ground lean beef	1 bell pepper, chopped	¼ tsp. powdered thyme
1 lb. chicken livers	2 stalks celery, chopped	1 bay leaf
1 large onion, chopped	3 shallots, chopped	2 cups canned chicken broth

Cook chicken livers, cool and grind. In a heavy pan cook ground beef in oil until light brown; stir often. Add onions, bell pepper and celery, cooking over medium heat until onions are transparent, then add salt, red pepper, thyme, bay leaf and chicken broth. Simmer for 30 minutes on low heat and then add the chicken livers just before removing from heat, mixing well. There should be about ½ cup liquid remaining in pan. Remove bay leaf. Combine freshly steamed rice with the hot meat mixture and blend well. Add shallots after removing from heat. Cover tightly and let stand 30 minutes. Heat before serving.

Spiced Hamburgers

1 tbsp. oleo	1 tsp. sugar
1 lb. ground beef	1 tsp. chili powder
1 large onion, chopped	1 can tomato sauce
1 dill pickle, chopped	½ tsp. salt

Melt oleo in heavy frying pan and cook beef patties (8) until light brown on both sides. Now add onion, dill pickle, sugar and chili powder. Cook for six minutes. Add tomato sauce and simmer for a few minutes. Serve on circles of toast with the gravy over the meat.

Bayou Hash

1 lb. ground beef	1 tsp. chili powder
3 tbsp. shortening	1 tsp. salt; 1 tsp. pepper
½ cup raw rice	2 large onions,
2½ cups cooked tomatoes	chopped

In a heavy pan brown onions in shortening, add meat, brown well. Add remaining in-gredients, cover pan. Over slow fire cook about 40 min., stirring occasionally. Serves 4.

Sour Cream Chops

6 pork chops	1 tsp. paprika
1½ cups onion slices	½ tsp. salt
1 garlic clove, minced	½ cup water
1 tsp. dill seed	1 cup sour cream

Brown chops on both sides in hot shorten-ing. Lower heat and add onions, garlic, dill seed, paprika, salt and water. Cover and cook for 60 minutes, or till tender. Stir in one cup sour cream and make a gravy. Simmer about 8 minutes. Serves 6.

Veal ~ Stuffed Pocket

Veal Roast	1 tsp. salt
8 slices bread	2 onions, chopped fine
shortening	1 bell pepper, chopped fine
flour	1 tsp. "Season All"

Toast bread and crumble. In hot shortening brown flour, stirring well. Add other ingredients and cook, stirring, 5 min. Cut pocket in roast and stuff well; sew up. Put in 350°F. oven, bast-ing often, until done. (about 30 min. per lb.)

Curried Beef and Avocado on toast

1 jar (5 ounces) sliced dried beef
1/4 cup chopped onion
1/4 cup butter or margarine
1/4 cup flour
1 tsp. curry powder

2 1/2 cups milk
2 medium ripe avocados, peeled
Lemon juice
12 slices hot toast, buttered
6 fresh fruit kabobs

Cover dried beef with boiling water and drain immediately. Tear dried beef into bite-size pieces. Sauté onion in butter (margarine) until tender, not brown. Blend in flour and curry powder. Add milk and cook slowly until sauce is thickened, stirring constantly. Stir beef into sauce and heat. Cut avocados in half lengthwise; remove pits. Cut each avocado half into three lengthwise slices and brush with lemon juice. Place half of the toast slices on serving plates and arrange three avocado slices on each slice of toast. Spoon dried beef mixture over avocado. Cut remaining toast slices into toast points. Garnish plates with toast points, fresh fruit kabobs, and parsley or mint. (serves 6).

(Special aside:)
Tomato juice served with a fleck of
curry powder has real masculine appeal.

Rosy Baked Ham

5 lb. fully cooked ham
1 cup crabapple jelly
1/3 cup sugar   dash of allspice
1/3 cup water   dash of salt
          1 tbsp. horseradish

Bake ham and meanwhile
prepare sauce. Combine jelly,
sugar, water, horseradish,
allspice, and salt in saucepan.
Heat and simmer one minute.
Remove ham from oven, turn heat
to 275°F. Brush top and sides
with crabapple sauce. Return
ham to oven and heat another
30 minutes, brushing ham again
with sauce 15 minutes before
removing from oven. Slice and
serve with candied apple rings,
and, if desired, any remaining
sauce. This will give you 20-24
slices of ham; about 1⅓ cups sauce.

Louisiana Brisket

3 lbs. brisket of beef, lean
3 carrots, sliced
1 onion, cut in half
1½ tsp. salt
Red and black pepper to taste
1 cup celery, chopped with leaves

Place brisket in kettle; add the
vegetables, salt and pepper. Add
boiling water to cover meat,
cover kettle and simmer three to
four hours until meat is tender. Add
a little water when necessary. When
done, remove meat to a hot platter.
The broth can be saved and stored
for future use. Slice brisket across
grain and serve with a simple
horseradish sauce made as
follows:

     to one part prepared
     horseradish add two parts
     tomato ketchup and blend.

Sausage Royale

½ pound good smoked sausage, cut in ½ inch thick rounds

1 small onion, chopped

1 small bell pepper, chopped

1 stalk celery, chopped

1 cup raw rice

1 tsp. salt

2 cups water

Fry sausage rounds, in own fat, over low heat, until slightly browned. Drain sausage on paper towels. Pour all fat from saucepan except 3 tablespoons. Sauté onion, celery and bell pepper in same pan until wilted, not brown. Add 2 cups water and one teaspoon salt. Bring to a boil and cook for two minutes. Remove from fire, add sausage and raw rice. Now pour all into a greased casserole with a tight fitting lid, cover and bake at 350°F. for 45 minutes.

MURIEL'S PEPPER JELLY

(for all meats) ▪ ⅛ to ¼ cup crushed red pepper (may be purchased in jars) ▪ ¾ cup chopped bell pepper ▪ 1½ cups apple cider ▪ 1 cup apple cider VINEGAR ▪ 6½ cups sugar ▪ 1½ btls. Certo (6½ oz.) ▪ red or green coloring ▪ COOK all ingredients, except Certo and color, to hard, rolling, boil. Boil 1 min., remove from heat, strain, add Certo and color, stir well and pour into 8, ½ pint, jelly jars.

Muriel says:

"c'est piquant le Diable avec la douceur d'un Ange!"

Peppered Chuck Steak with Burgundy

3 pounds chuck beef	2 bell peppers	¾ cup dry red wine
flour	3 medium size onions	1 bay leaf
salt and pepper	1 No 2 can tomatoes	parsley – few sprigs
¼ cup cooking oil	1 can tomato paste, small	green celery tops

Cover meat thoroughly with flour and pound with meat pounder. Brown on both sides in oil, then place steak in a roasting pan. Spread over steak bell peppers, sliced, onions sliced thin and them combine tomatoes and tomato paste and pour over steak. Season with salt and pepper to taste. Add wine, parsley, chopped celery tops and the bay leaf. Bring to a boil, cover tightly and bake in a 350°F. oven at least 2 hrs.

Spanish Meat Pie

3 cups diced meat ⟶ beef, veal, pork, or a combination of any or all ⟵		
3 tbsp. olive oil	1 tbsp. flour	1½ cup water
1 small onion, minced	¼ cup green olives, sliced	1 tsp. salt
1 tbsp. minced parsley	¼ cup mushrooms, drained	Pastry

Sauté meat in oil, add onion and parsley. Slowly add water and simmer. Stir once or twice and when smooth remove from heat; add olives and mushrooms. Line a baking dish with pastry and pour in meat filling, then top with pastry; cut large gashes in top crust. Brush crust with olive oil and bake at 350°F. until golden brown; about 45 minutes.
Six to eight servings.

GAME

FRIED RABBIT

1 young rabbit   1/8 tsp. paprika
1/2 cup flour   1/2 cup drippings
2 tsp. salt   red pepper to taste

Wash rabbit, dry thoroughly and cut into pieces. Dredge with flour to which seasonings have been added. Heat drippings in frying pan and add rabbit. Keep heat up, but not smoking, until rabbit pieces a golden brown all over. Reduce flame and cook slowly about 30 or 45 minutes depending on size of rabbit. Serve with a cream gravy.

SQUIRREL

Squirrel meat is similar to rabbit but more delicate in flavor. A medium size squirrel makes about two servings. Cook as directed for rabbit. The meat is quite lean. If roasted, cover with strips salt pork.

RABBIT JAMBALAYA

Wash rabbit, dry thoroughly and cut into pieces. Dredge in flour seasoned with salt and pepper. Sear in hot grease, add minced shallots, diced bell peppers and enough stock (can be made with chicken or beef bouillon cubes) to cover. Simmer for one hour or until almost done. Now add two cups of washed, uncooked rice. Cook for 30 minutes or 'till rice is done.

Broiled Game Birds

Tender young birds may be split and broiled like chicken. Brush with plenty of butter and baste frequently. Broiling time depends on size of bird and how well done you like the meat.

Quail: 10 to 15 minutes
Grouse: 15 to 20 minutes
Young partridge and pheasant: 20-30 min.

for your personal notes and good recipes

Time table *for* Cooking Most Meats:
Beef: rare, 15 minutes per pound; well done, about 20 minutes.
Fowls: 20 minutes per pound on the average. (Game birds, see page 45).
Lamb: 30 minutes per pound   Pork: 30 minutes per pound.
Veal: 30 minutes per pound.

Poultry and Duck
volaille et canard

Breaded Fried Chicken with Creole Gravy

1 large fryer, 2 to 3 pounds	½ cup stale bread crumbs, or more
½ cup flour, more if needed	salt and pepper
1 egg	"Season-All"
2 tbsp. milk	cooking oil

Cut chicken into serving pieces and rub thoroughly with "Season-All." Use a heavy frying pan with enough oil to cover chicken pieces. Roll chicken in seasoned flour and dip in the well beaten egg and milk mixture. Now roll in bread crumbs and cook over a hot fire until all sides are a golden brown. Remove from pan to a warm plate and hold until gravy is prepared. Have the following ingredients ready to use: 1 tbsp. finely chopped celery – 1 tsp. paprika – ½ cup milk – 2 tbsp. flour – ½ cup canned chicken broth. When all chicken is removed from the fire, immediately put the diced celery in the hot pan, reduce heat and cook for 5 to 6 minutes. Add flour, stirring often, then stir in chicken broth and milk. Cook for 5 minutes over low to medium flame and stirring until gravy is smooth

---

Creole cooking's a blend of the finest French, Spanish, Negro and Indian skills~it antedates American Independence. A gift from old world Louisiana to grace your table.

48

Chicken Fricassee

1 large, young, hen   2 tbsp. flour
3 large onions   red pepper to taste
1 heaping tbsp. shortening — salt

Cut chicken as for frying. Chop onions very fine. Brown chicken in hot shortening; remove from pan. Place flour in hot pan, stirring until light brown. Add onions and cook until mixture is golden brown. Now add chicken and a quart of boiling water. Season with salt and pepper and when almost done add some shallot tops and parsley. Stir occasionally as stew thickens to prevent burning. A can of mushrooms can now be added if desired. Serve with Dumplings added about 12 minutes before serving, dropping them in gently and bringing pot to a brisk boil. Dumplings: sift 2 cups flour, 3 tsp. baking powder and ½ tsp. salt; add one cup milk slowly, stirring until batter is smooth.

Chicken à la king

2 cups cooked chicken pepper
4 ounces butter   1 bell pepper, chopped
4 tbsp. flour   ½ cup sliced mushrooms
1 cup chicken broth   2 egg yolks
 salt   2 tbsp. pimentos, chopped
½ cup coffee cream 3 oz. dry wine (optional)

Make a white sauce melting 2 oz. butter in saucepan; blend in 4 tbsp. flour, add chicken broth and cream, cooking slowly and stirring constantly. When sauce has thickened add salt and pepper to taste, and the two cups of coarsely chopped chicken. In another pan melt 2 oz. of butter, then add bell pepper and mushrooms. When these are tender, add to cream sauce and chicken. Simmer and stir lightly for about ten minutes, then add two lightly beaten egg yolks, stirring constantly for about one minute over low heat. Remove from heat, add pimentos (and wine if used), mix and serve hot.

Chicken in Skillet – lucie

1 large fryer, cut-up	salt and pepper
3 tbsp. oil or oleo	"Season-All"
2 tbsp. flour	½ onion, sliced
1 stalk celery	1 can chicken broth

Roll chicken pieces in seasoned flour (salt, pepper, "Season-All"). Melt oil in an Electric skillet and add chicken, turning and browning lightly all over. Separate onion slices into rings and place over chicken. Add the celery cut into strips. Now pour one-half of chicken broth into skillet and turn heat control to low. Cook for one hour with cover on skillet. During this period add the remaining half can of broth.

Chicken and Broccoli

An interesting variation of the recipe given below: place slices of cooked chicken on buttered toast and cover with a whole spear of cooked broccoli. Pour the hot poulette sauce over the broccoli and chicken. Run under broiler flame until lightly brown. A very good luncheon dish with a molded fruit salad.

Turkey Poulette – lucie

For each individual serving ⟵⟶
Place a triangle slice of buttered toast in an oven-ware platter. On top of the toast put a thin slice of boiled ham and cover with slices of turkey. Over all pour the poulette: a seasoned white sauce containing a goodly amount of sharp cheddar cheese. Place under the broiler flame and leave until top is a light brown.

Chicken Casserole

2 large broilers   garlic salt
2 cups water   flour
½ tsp. salt   ⅓ cup butter
2 stalks celery   pepper
2 carrots, chopped   2 small onions
1 can evaporated milk

Cut up chicken and put in pot with water, salt and vegetables. Bring to a boil and simmer, covered, 30 minutes, or until chicken is almost tender. Remove from broth and cool. Remove meat in large pieces from bones. Add one tsp. garlic salt to ¼ cup flour and dredge chicken with this mixture; brown in hot oil. Remove chicken meat to a casserole. Blend 1½ tbsp. flour in skillet drippings and season with garlic salt and pepper to taste. When flour is a golden brown pour this over chicken. Cover casserole and put in a 350°F. oven for 15 minutes. Four servings.

Chicken Avocado

Split avocado and remove seed. Fill the cavity with creamed chicken or turkey. Run into the oven until the avocado is thoroughly heated. A delicious luncheon dish preparable before-hand.

Chicken Sandwich

1 hen   3 eggs, hard boiled, cut fine
1 tsp. capers   3 sour gherkins
salt and pepper   1 cup celery, chopped

Boil chicken in sufficient hot water to cook. Add two garlic cloves and when meat is very tender season with salt and pepper. Cut white meat very fine, grind dark meat, pickles and capers, then mix with celery and eggs. Add one cup chicken broth and enough mayonnaise to hold mix together and spread mixture not too thick. Decorate top with thin slices of stuffed olives.

Chicken Sauce Piquant

1 4 to 5 pound hen, disjointed	1 can whole, peeled, Italian tomatoes
1½ cups celery, diced	1 garlic clove, crushed
1 cup shallot tops, diced	1 cup mushrooms
1 onion, chopped	1 can small, green, peas

Dredge chicken pieces in seasoned flour. Cover bottom of heavy pot with melted shortening. Brown chicken quickly over hot fire; remove chicken. Clean pot of all fat and browned flour. Replace one-half cup of this fat, free of flour, in pot and heat. Add about 3 tablespoons of fresh flour and stir well until a light brown. Add onions and cook slowly over low heat about 3 minutes, or until onions are wilted—not brown. Now add celery and let this wilt about one minute. Add about one pint of boiling water and cook, stirring well, until all is blended. Put chicken pieces in this gravy and add tomatoes. Cover pot and cook over slow to medium heat about one and one-half hours. Check chicken meat and if it starts falling from bones, remove chicken pieces and, if necessary, continue cooking sauce until thoroughly blended. Season while cooking with salt, pepper and a dash or two of worcester sauce. Just before removing from fire, add mushrooms with their liquor and drained peas and cook just to heat, stirring well. Watch the sauce and do not permit it to thicken too much, but you do want it rather thick. Serve with hot, steamed rice, and any tossed, green, salad. Try slicing a French loaf _thin_ with garlic butter.

Turkey and Eggplant *de España*

6 slices turkey breast
1 large eggplant
2 slices baked ham
2 tbsp. olive oil
1 garlic clove, minced
1 can tomato paste
1½ cups cream
½ cup turkey gravy

Cut eggplant in thin slices and brown with garlic in olive oil. Drain on paper towel, then place eggplant slices in large, shallow, baking dish. Cover eggplant with slices of turkey, then a layer of eggplant and sprinkle with salt and pepper. Next put in a layer of thin ham slices and top with a layer of eggplant. Season top with salt and pepper. Now mix thoroughly the tomato paste, cream the turkey gravy and pour over layers of eggplant, turkey and ham. Bake in a 350°F. oven for about thirty minutes.

Breast of Wild Duck

sliced breast of a roast duck
gravy from duck
10 ripe olives, chopped
¼ cup shallots, chopped
2 tbsp. butter
½ cup sherry wine
1 tbsp. lemon juice
salt and pepper
thyme and basil, a pinch each

Heat the butter over low heat and sauté shallots until wilted. Add duck slices and remaining ingredients. Bring sauce to a boil, lower heat, and simmer gently for 5 to 8 minutes. Serve on slice: buttered toast.

"Bayou Cooking," at the start of this book, tells in simple layman's language what herbs and spices are and how and when to use them.

Ducks in Orange Wine

4 small wild ducks
1 tsp. worcester sauce
5 drops pepper sauce
2 cups orange (or sweet) wine
½ pound butter
salt

In a heavy pot, over low heat, melt the butter and add the ducks, increase to medium heat, browning ducks. Add sauces, wine and salt. Cook slowly until ducks are tender and the wine and natural juices have cooked down to a gravy consistency. Serve on a platter with mounds of wild rice. Put the gravy in a gravy boat. (Long grain rice may be used in place of wild rice. If desired, substitute orange juice for wine)

French Wild Ducks

Wild ducks, quartered, ½ bell pepper
salt and red pepper   very dry red wine
shortening   1 large onion, each duck

Season duck quarters thoroughly with salt and red pepper. Cover bottom of heavy pot with shortening and brown duck quarters well on both sides. While duck is browning, chop up onion and bell pepper in amount desired for number of ducks cooked. When duck is quite brown, add onion and bell pepper to pot, cover pot and cook at low heat, without water, in own juice. When the onions are well cooked and a light brown, add the wine according to the amount of gravy desired. Continue cooking until duck is tender.

"We may live without friends, we may live without books,
But civilized man cannot live without cooks."
 - Owen Meredith -

Turkey Loaf

3 cups soft bread crumbs
6 tsp. butter
2½ cups chicken broth
2 tbsp. onion, finely chopped
½ cup celery, finely chopped
¼ cup chopped pimento
4 eggs slightly beaten
3 cups cooked turkey, diced
salt and pepper

Mix all ingredients well and shape into
a loaf. Place in a well greased baking
dish. Have a pan of hot water in the oven,
set at 325°F., and place the baking dish
in the hot water. Bake about 45
minutes, or until the loaf is firm.

Southern Chicken Pie

5 tbsp. butter   2½ cups cooked
1 onion, sliced   chicken pieces
4 tbsp. flour   2 cups ham, diced
2 cups chicken broth - celery and onion salt

Heat butter over low heat in heavy
pan, add onions and cook until wilted.
Add flour and stir until blended. Then
slowly add chicken broth and stir over
low heat until thick and smooth. Season
to taste with salt and pepper, onion and
celery salts. Arrange chicken meat in
layers with diced ham in large casserole,
or in six ramekins. Cover with sauce. Top
with biscuits, toasted bread crumbs or
pastry. Bake in 425°F. oven for about 20 min.

Chicken Jambalaya

1 very large fryer (3 or 4 lbs.)
2 tbsp. cooking oil
2 tbsp. bacon drippings
1 tbsp. salt
½ tsp. red pepper
½ cup celery, chopped
½ cup bell pepper, chopped
1 large onion, chopped

1 garlic clove, minced
¼ cup parsley, minced
¼ shallot tops, minced
2 cups raw rice
5 cups water
6 chicken bouillon cubes
1 bay leaf
¼ tsp. powdered thyme

Season cut-up chicken with salt and pepper. In a heavy pot heat the oil and the bacon drippings, then brown chicken using medium heat. Remove chicken pieces to another pan. Cook onions, celery and bell peppers in the heavy pot until wilted-not brown. Add water, chicken bouillon cubes, thyme, garlic and bay leaf. Bring to a boil and boil briskly for 15 minutes. There should be some four cups of liquid after boiling. While liquid is cooking down, remove chicken meat from bones in as large pieces as possible. Remove pot from fire and add the chicken meat, parsley, shallots and raw rice. Mix lightly. Place in a casserole, or leave in Dutch oven chicken was browned in. Leave bay leaf on top. Cover tightly and bake for two hours: the _First_ hour at 375°F. and the _Second_ hour at 350°F. Remove bay leaf and serve. A truly Deep South Louisiana dish — delicious.

Extra Special

Margaret Shaffer's APPLE CAKE from Ardoyne Plantation.

1½ cups Wesson oil	3 cups plain flour	1 tsp. cinnamon
2½ cups sugar	1 tsp. salt	3 cups apples, finely
2 eggs	1 tsp. soda	diced
2 tsp. vanilla	1 tsp. nutmeg	1 cup. pecans, chopped

Cream oil and sugar; add vanilla and eggs. Now add dry ingredients alternately with the apples and pecans. Place mixture in a greased and floured tube cake pan and bake one hour at 350°F. When removed from oven run a knife edge down sides of cake while _hot_ and immediately apply glaze letting glaze run down sides of cake. Cool cake com_plete_ly before removing from cake pan.

For the G_laze_, mix 1½ cups powdered sugar and 6 tsp. lemon juice until smooth and apply to cake as above.

(This recipe and cake arrived as we are going to the printers so is placed here. APPLE CAKE is just too good not to be included.)

a_good basic recipe_ ↪ Be a little limber, Be a little loony. Be a little loving, Eat a little lightly and you'll live a long, long, life — Lucie says.

↪hasn't this been fun so far?

VEGETABLES and EGGS

French Fried Asparagus

Asparagus - *freshly cooked or canned.*
2 tbsp. cream - 2 tbsp. flour - 1 egg
Prepare batter of cream, flour and egg,
mixing until smooth. Drain asparagus
well and roll in batter. Fry in a saucepan with butter or oil at 380°F. until
done. *(At 380°F. a cube of bread turns light
brown in 35 to 40 seconds).*

Chopped Spinach

1 pkg. frozen chopped spinach
Cook spinach as directed on package.
Make a white sauce blending flour in
hot oil and slowly adding milk to the
consistency desired. Add one beaten
egg and ½ cup grated cheese to seasoned sauce and fold into spinach. Place all
in buttered baking dish, top with bread
crumbs, dots of butter, bake at 350°F. until crumbs are brown.

Red Beans and Rice

3 cups dried red beans
1 ham bone with plenty of meat
1 tbsp. cooking oil 1 garlic clove, minced
1 tbsp. flour   1 sprig parsley
1 onion, diced   4 shallots, minced
        red pepper
Heat oil in deep pot over low fire. Add
flour, as for a roux, onions and garlic.
Stir frequently and cook till light brown.
Add the ham bone with meat and put
in beans, adding water to cover beans.
Cook slowly, stirring often, until beans
are tender - about one to one and a half
hours. Serve over hot, cooked, rice
with the minced shallots on top -
*a real Southern dish served often in
many local homes.*

Sweet Potatoes & Orange

2 oranges
4 sweet potatoes, large
2 tbsp. orange rind, grated
1/3 cup orange pulp, chopped
1/2 tsp. cinnamon ~ 1/2 cup butter ~ 1 tsp. salt
Have ready: the sweet potatoes
boiled, the butter melted, orange
rind and orange pulp. Peel and mash
sweet potatoes, heat in a pot, until
fluffy, together with all other
ingredients. Spoon mixture into a
baking dish or individual ramekins
and sprinkle with some orange rind.
Brown under the broiler and serve
hot. Serves six.

Corn Sauté with Peppers

6 ears of corn   2 shallots, minced
2 bell peppers   2 tbsp. butter
1 or 2 garlic cloves, minced
Cut corn kernels off cobs and chop
the bell peppers finely. Melt butter,
fry the shallots and garlic in it for
five minutes over low fire. Add corn and
bell pepper, salt and black pepper to taste.
Cook another five minutes and then
add two tablespoons of hot water,
cover pan closely, reduce heat and
simmer for fifteen minutes checking
water to prevent dryness. Just before
serving stir in the mixture, to melt
and mix, a tablespoon of butter.

In preparing vegetables a bowl and vegetable
choppers are always the best things to use,
for most varieties. Not so, parsley! Take the
parsley needed in one hand and snip as fine
or as coarse as desired with a pair of kitchen shears.

FRENCH FRIED BANANAS

bananas
corn flakes
eggs
cooking oil

Judge amounts each ingredient based on number of bananas used.

Cut bananas in desired sizes (split or in rounds) and dip in lightly beaten egg. Then cover all sides with finely crushed corn flakes. Have hot oil in saucepan to cover bananas. Fry at 380°F. (until a cube of bread turns light brown in 35 to 40 seconds) until golden brown. Serve as a vegetable with veal, pork chops or broiled lamb.

Asparagus Casserole

1 small can green asparagus tips
1 can cream of mushroom soup
4 eggs, hard boiled and cubed
¼ pound cheddar cheese, coarsely grated
12 saltine crackers, toasted and crumbled
salt and pepper to taste
1 cup milk

Butter casserole and place a layer of cracker crumbs on bottom. Add grated cheese, cubed eggs, asparagus and some soup. Repeat layers, dotting the top of each layer with black pepper and salt. Sprinkle top layer with crumbs and add milk to moisten. Bake at 350° F. 20 to 30 minutes until top crumbs are light brown.

Muriel says — try cooking artichokes with salt, wine vinegar and a couple of cloves of garlic added to the water. Dip the leaves in lemon butter seasoned with onion or garlic salt- or in mayonnaise so seasoned.

Barbecued Onions

1 large Bermuda onion
2 tbsp. barbecue sauce
4 tbsp. flour
1 tbsp. chili powder
1 tbsp. butter or oleo

Peel onion, cut off ends well down in
onion to get large slices, ¼ inch thick.
separate onion slices into rings, spread
well with barbecue, dust well with
flour on both sides and sprinkle
chili powder over both sides. Place
rings on greased, flat, biscuit sheet,
brush lightly with melted butter
or oleo and brown in broiler under
a medium flame until golden
brown, turning once only.

Tomato ~ Eggplant casserole

1 medium eggplant
½ in. boiling water
1½ tsp. salt
2 eggs, beaten
2 tbsp. butter or oleo
½ cup cheddar cheese, grated
¼ tsp. ground black pepper
1 tsp. finely chopped onion
½ tsp. oregano leaves
½ cup crumbled saltines
6 medium size tomato slices

Peel eggplant and cut slices ¼ in. thick.
Place in saucepan with boiling water and
salt. Cover; bring to boil, cook 10 min. or till
tender. Drain and mash. Blend butter (oleo),
egg, pepper, onion, oregano and saltines. Turn
into buttered 1 qt. casserole. Cover surface with
tomato slices and sprinkle with salt, black
pepper and cheese. Bake in 375°F. oven
25 min., or until lightly brown on top.

   and thanks to Disée

Spaghetti — Italian Style

3 medium size onions, chopped rather fine
3 tablespoons cooking oil
2 garlic cloves, minced
1 can tomato paste
1 pound ground meat, seasoned to taste

3 cans water (use tomato paste can)
1 tablespoon butter
salt and pepper to taste
parmesan cheese, grated, as needed
1 package fine spaghetti

Put oil in heavy skillet over medium heat, add onions and garlic. Cook until onions are wilted. Form meat in small balls and brown with onions. Add tomato paste, salt, pepper and a pinch of sugar. Slowly add hot water, stirring well, and continue cooking until sauce is thick and tasty. Have spaghetti cooking as directed on package. When ready to serve, drain and blend in the butter. Then mix with the spaghetti a small amount of sauce from skillet and pile on a platter or plate. Top with the sauce and meat balls, cover well – use plenty- with grated cheese. (It's always good to have a small bowl of grated cheese, for those who love it, on the table). Serve with hot garlic bread and a green salad.

Fried Okra

okra as needed ∖ salt, pepper ∖ 1 beaten egg ∖ cracker crumbs ∖ cooking oil as needed
Use small to medium size okra pods, wash, drain and season with salt and pepper. Roll the pods in the beaten egg, then cracker crumbs. Fry in hot, deep, fat until delicate brown. Drain on absorbent paper and serve as hot as possible.

62

CARROTS~GREEN BEANS and CELERY

½ pound carrots cut into 2"-2½" long strips
1 pkg. frozen French Style green beans.
1 cup celery, sliced diagonally, thin.
3 tbsp. butter or oleo
salt and pepper to taste

Boil carrot strips in a small amount of
of water, five minutes. Add celery, boil
five minutes more, then add green
beans and cook another five minutes.
Add salt, pepper and butter and cook
ten minutes over low heat until the
mixture is the consistency desired.
Adding one-quarter cup chopped
roasted almonds with the butter
enhances the flavor.

Note to All guests:
   Don't forget to kiss the cook
   (male or female!) after an
   enjoyable meal.

CRÉOLE BROWNED OKRA

2 large, firm, tomatoes, cut in small pieces
3 pounds okra, slice thin rings
1 large onion, chopped
3 tbsp. crisco
1 tsp. salt
⅛ tsp. cayenne pepper
1 tsp. lemon juice

Melt crisco in thick pot or skillet over
low heat and add okra. Brown lightly,
stirring frequently to prevent scorching.
Add lemon juice, to prevent okra "roping",
and chopped onion. Continue cooking
and stirring until mixture has cooked
down and is brown. Add tomato,
salt and pepper. Place cover on tightly
and steam ten minutes. To prevent okra
sticking to the pot, keep lifting cover
and turning with a spatula -

CAULIFLOWER au GRATIN

One cauliflower
sharp cheddar cheese, grated
milk as needed
two tablespoons butter
three tablespoons flour
salt and pepper

Soak cauliflower in cold, salted, water for fifteen minutes. Then plunge into boiling water, slightly salted. Boil the cauliflower until just tender (do not overcook!) drain and break off sprigs. Now prepare a cream sauce using the butter, flour and milk. (When the flour is blended smoothly with the butter, melted, add milk slowly, constantly stirring, until the sauce is the consistency you desire.) Place the cauliflower in a baking dish, add grated cheese and the cream sauce seasoned with salt and pepper. Sprinkle plenty grated cheese and dots of butter over top of sauce. Bake until brown at 350°F.

Irish potatoes, cabbage and turnips are delicious prepared in this same manner.

64

Green Beans with Cheese

2 cans green beans
1 can cream of mushroom soup
⅓ cup sliced almonds
½ cup grated cheese
½ tsp. salt
½ tsp. pepper
3 tbsp. butter

Mix together the drained beans, soup, cheese, salt and pepper. Pour into a buttered baking dish. Cover the top with sliced almonds and dot well with butter. Bake at 350°F. for 30 minutes.

For perfect steamed rice (p.66) Wearever Aluminum makes a "Rice Cooker". This can be used in many other ways and with this utensil in your kitchen you'll never again hesitate to prepare rice.

Savory Baked Beans

2 cans Boston Style beans
1 cup canned tomatoes
1 onion, chopped
½ green pepper, chopped
¼ stick oleo
¼ cup molasses
1 tsp. dry mustard
2 tsp. worcester sauce

Cook onion and green pepper in oleo until wilted and add the other seasonings and tomatoes, mixing thoroughly. Add the mixture to the beans and stir gently to combine well. Bake in a greased casserole, uncovered, for one hour, or until excess liquid has cooked out.

Every good Barbecue deserves Baked Beans.

STUFFED EGGPLANT Oaklawn Gardens

2 medium size eggplant
½ pound ground, lean beef
1 small bell pepper, chopped
2 onions, chopped
1 garlic clove, cut fine

4 slices bacon
1 tbsp. worcester sauce
3 slices stale or toasted bread, soaked
    in water or milk and squeezed dry.
Bread crumbs, small amount.

Boil eggplants until tender, about 10 minutes. Remove, cool and cut into two parts. Then scrape out inside leaving about ½ inch lining. Broil bacon in dry skillet until crisp, taking great care not to burn bacon or fat. Reserve bacon and in remaining fat fry onions, bell pepper, garlic, until onion is light brown. Add bacon, broken in pieces, and the meat, then worcester sauce and cook a few minutes, stirring to blend ingredients. Now add the mashed eggplant and soft bread and season to taste with salt, pepper, chopped green onion tops and parsley. Fry mixture awhile longer, then fill eggplant shells, cover with bread crumbs, dot with butter and brown in oven at 375°F.

Variations: Use shrimp, boiled and in pieces, ham, chicken livers or gizzards for the meat. 1 cup of mushrooms can be browned with the onions and bell peppers. Parmeson cheese, finely prepared, can be substituted on top.

RICE ~~~

an important staple of Creole cooking. Many of our new residents from up North are used to rice as a cereal or dessert (puddings). Thus they usually serve sticky, even "gooey," grains. So - to get rice cooked 'till done, fluffy and with separate grains, we'll continue.

STEAMED RICE

2 cups long grain rice   3 cups water   1 tsp. salt   1 tsp. vinegar   ½ tsp. oil

For best results use a heavy aluminum pot with close fitting lid. Place all ingredients in pot and cook, uncovered, over fairly high flame until water is just about all cooked out. (This takes about 8 minutes. If cooking 1 cup rice and 1½ cups water, 6 minutes should do.) DO NOT STIR. Now lower fire to simmer or your lowest flame, put an asbestos lid under the pot, cover tightly and steam for 30 minutes without stirring. If your fire is low enough the rice should never burn and each grain should be tender but not gummy. (Short grain rice takes less water: 1 cup rice to 1 cup water.)

Helpful hints: Don't soak rice before cooking – Don't moisten rice and leave wet for a long time before cooking – When tossing or fluffing cooked rice, use a fork, not a spoon – One cup raw rice, cooked, will give 4 to 6 normal servings – Serve steamed rice with: (1) any gravy [roast, chicken, steak, duck or turkey] (2) shrimp creole and curried shrimp (3) chili [put scoop in each bowl of chili] (4) any gumbo [a scoop in each bowl] (5) any stew [shrimp, chicken or meat].

EGGS — des oeufs

Eggs with Spinach

1 package-frozen chopped spinach
white cream sauce (butter, flour, milk)
grated parmesan cheese
2 eggs ——— butter

Boil spinach as directed on package, drain well, add some butter. Poach the eggs, adding salt and pepper to taste. Put one tablespoon butter in pyrex pan, add spinach. Place eggs on top of the spinach, cover with the cream sauce, add grated cheese.

a Southern Fluffy Omelet

4 eggs   2 tbsp. boiling water
1/4 tsp. salt   butter as needed

Beat eggs separately, adding salt to yolks, until very light, then combine whites and yolks. Melt butter in hot skillet, but do not brown, and pour in egg mixture. Pour about two tablespoons of boiling water over the eggs and, when done, fold the omelet with two cake turners and serve at once.

- les oeufs -
Pickle them; Fry them; Boil them; Bake them!
use them raw - poached - fried - hard cooked - soft boiled!
(and — they're inexpensive, besides!)

68

Cajun Cheese Casserole

½ lb. mild cheddar cheese, sliced thin
2 eggs
6 slices of bread
1 cup milk
dash of white pepper
½ tsp. salt
butter

Place two bread slices in buttered baking dish and top with half the cheese slices. Place two more bread slices over this and add remaining cheese. Top with last two bread slices. Beat eggs, add milk, pepper, salt and pour over bread in baking dish. Dot with butter and bake at 325°F. for about thirty minutes.

Scrambled Eggs Special

1 cup cooked rice
1 tbsp. parsley, chopped
¼ cup cooked ham, chopped
3 tbsp. crisco or oleo
1 egg, well beaten
2 tbsp. water
salt and pepper to taste

In a heavy skillet melt crisco and slowly warm rice, water, parsley and ham. Add well beaten egg and seasoning to rice, stirring until egg is done. Serve immediately — Serves two.

Poached Eggs Creole

Put about ¾ inch water in a shallow pan and bring to a slow boil. Break each egg into a saucer, sprinkle with salt and pepper and a touch of finely minced parsley. Slip from saucer into water, cover, reduce heat and let stand about five minutes until set.

Country Store Pickled Eggs

12 hard-cooked eggs	1 tsp. salt
2 cups white vinegar	2 tbsp. pickling spices
2 tbsp. sugar	1 onion, sliced
	2 pods sliced garlic

Combine all ingredients, except eggs, in qt. of water and simmer 5 minutes. Place eggs, (shelled eggs) in a jar and cover with pickling liquid. Let stand for several days before using.

Scrambled Eggs with Eggplant

4 eggs	4 tsp. milk
½ eggplant diced	½ cup flour
2 tsp. salt	¼ tsp. paprika
4 tsp. butter	dash pepper

Mix flour, one teaspoon salt and paprika. Dry eggplant and roll in seasoned flour. Melt butter in saucepan and sauté eggplant until tender and brown. Beat eggs with milk, pepper and remaining salt. Add to eggplant and cook, stirring occasionally until done. Serves six.

Shrimp Omelet

1 pound raw, cleaned, shrimp
2 tbsp. oleo
1 tbsp. bell pepper, minced
1 tbsp. prepared horseradish
2 tbsp. flour
2 cans tomato sauce
   pepper sauce
6 eggs

Sauté shrimp in oleo until pink. Add onion and pepper and cook until soft, not brown. Blend in horseradish and flour. Add tomato sauce and pepper sauce and cook over low heat, stirring frequently, five to ten minutes until thickened. Cook omelet and pour some sauce inside before turning one half over. Place omelet on platter and then pour remaining sauce over finished omelet Serve hot and have plenty hot biscuits ready!

for your personal notes and recipes

Have water _boiling_ when
you add fresh vegetables. Cold water
can toughen them. Cook until just tender.

Salads : Biscuits : Breads

Summer Salad

6 ripe tomatoes
3 cucumbers
3 bell peppers
1 onion, medium size
1 cup mayonnaise
2 packages cream cheese~3 ounce size
1 tbsp. plain gelatine
¼ cup cold water
  salt and cayenne to taste

Chop the vegetables very fine, drain
and salt. Blend mayonnaise with cream
cheese and add cayenne. Soak gelatine
in cold water, dissolve over hot water.
When cool, add to mayonnaise and
cream cheese. Stir this mixture and
the vegetables together carefully,
pour into molds, and place in
refrigerator to set. Serve cold on crisp
lettuce.

Avocado Salad

Cut ripe avocados in halves and remove
seed. Remove meat with a teaspoon and
mix with small pieces of fresh tomatoes.
Season the mayonnaise with worcester
sauce and grated onion. Mix well with
avocado and let marinate a few minutes.
Place the mixture in the avocado shells
and chill. Serve on lettuce leaf.

Basic French Dressing

⅓ cup lemon juice 1 tsp. paprika
1 cup olive oil ½ tsp. sugar
¼ tsp. pepper pinch of cayenne
1 tsp. salt see below, some variations

Combine all ingredients. Shake or beat
until thoroughly combined - chill. Shake
very well each time before using. Makes
1-⅓ cups. For a good garlic flavor, add
½ garlic clove, finely crushed to above.
— and vary your dressings easily—

Roquefort dressing : Add 4 tablespoons
crumbled Roquefort ("blue") cheese. For
green salads and tomato salad.

Horseradish Dressing : Add 2 tablespoons horse-radish. For meats.

Anchovy dressing : Add 2 tablespoons
anchovy paste and 1½ tablespoons of
each of the following—minced parsley
and chives. For green salads.

Chicken Salad

1 chicken
½ cup celery, cut fine
4 hard-boiled eggs, chopped
1 dill pickle, chopped small
  a few capers, to taste
½ cup chicken broth
1 garlic clove

Boil chicken until tender in water with
garlic clove, salt and red pepper.
Remove meat from bones, cut into
medium size pieces with scissors. Add
the chicken broth, then add celery,
chopped egg, pickles and capers. Let
stand in refrigerator to chill thoroughly
Add mayonnaise to taste and serve
on lettuce. Vary with one cup toasted
almonds or one-half cup diced
cucumbers or one cup cubed, cooked ham,
added to the above.

Shrimp Salad

1 pound cooked, deveined shrimp
1 cup celery, coarsely chopped
2 hard-boiled eggs, coarsely chopped.
2 tbsp. dill pickles, minced
  mayonnaise
1 tbsp. catsup
½ tsp. worcester sauce
  salt and pepper to taste
If shrimp are large, cut in halves or
quarters. Mix shrimp, celery, eggs, and
pickles together lightly with mayonnaise
to which has been added the catsup,
worcester sauce, salt and pepper.
Serve on torn lettuce leaves, (washed
and dried) and garnish with tomato
slices.

Italian Tossed Salad

1 head endive
½ head lettuce
1 medium tomato
8 black olives
8 stuffed olives
1 small can anchovies
Wash and tear greens. Dry thoroughly
Cut tomatoes in cubes. Chop the
olives and anchovies. Prepare the
following dressing beforehand
and mix well with salad ingredients
  4 tbsp. olive oil
  Juice of one lemon
  dash of salad herbs
  ¼ tsp. garlic salt
  ¼ tsp. onion salt
  ¼ tsp. celery salt
  ¼ tsp. salt
  ¼ tsp. black or white pepper
Garnish salad with whole
anchovies or olives.

Avocado and Fruit Salad

Avocado
  Grapefruit sections
    Orange sections
      Romaine lettuce
        water cress

For each serving use 4 wedges of avocado
meat, alternating with 3 grapefruit
sections and 3 orange sections. Arrange
on long leaves of romaine lettuce.
Garnish with water cress on the side
and serve with:

— fruit French dressing —

¼ cup orange juice
¼ cup pineapple juice
2 tbsp. lemon juice
  ¼ cup olive oil
  ¼ tsp. salt
  1 tsp sugar
Combine all ingredients, shake until well blended. Makes one cup. *For all fruit salads*.

Potato Salad

3 cups potatoes, sliced
3 tbsp. onion, grated
1 tbsp. lemon juice
1 tbsp. prepared mustard
½ cup pickles, dill or sweet (your choice)
          chopped
4 hard-boiled eggs, chopped
  mayonnaise ← ⅓ cup French dress-
  salt and pepper to taste   ing

Mix potatoes, onion, lemon juice, mustard,
pickles and eggs. Then add French dressing. Chill for several hours. Before
serving add enough mayonnaise to
moisten. Season to taste and serve in
lettuce cups. — six servings —

*Vary your potato salad by using
one cup of either chopped ripe olives
or sliced stuffed olives in place of
the chopped pickle.*

<u>Avocado Salad</u> - with Shrimp

1 avocado	2 stuffed olives, minced
1 pound cleaned, cooked shrimp	1 tbsp. celery, chopped fine
3 pickled onions	½ tsp. shrimp cocktail sauce

Remove avocado meat and mash fine (lightly). Mix the onions, celery, olives and cocktail sauce with the shrimp that's been diced. Combine well with avocado meat and serve in mounds on crisp lettuce. Add a bit more sauce to each serving, if desired.

<u>Mock Hollandaise Sauce</u> ~ lucie

Gently melt ½ stick oleo in saucepan. Remove from fire and add 4 tbsp. mayonnaise, mixing thoroughly together. Add one whole egg and combine well. Now stir in lemon juice to taste and a few grains of salt. Heat gently over very low fire. Serve at once.

<u>Luncheon Suggestion</u>:   Marinated Shrimp on lettuce ~
a mound of chopped spinach, ½ hard boiled
egg with Hollandaise sauce on top and
hot rolls Fruit or cake ~ iced tea

In the center of a plate place a mound of seasoned, chopped spinach, very well drained. On top of spinach mound, place half of a hard boiled egg, unsliced. Spoon Mock Hollandaise Sauce over all.

Beet Salad

1 pkg. lemon jello
1 cup boiling water
¾ cup water in which beets were boiled
3 tbsp. vinegar
½ tsp. salt
2 tsp. onion juice
1 tbsp. horseradish
¾ cups diced celery
1 cup cooked beets, diced

Dissolve jello with boiling water. Add beet water, vinegar, salt, onion juice, and horse-radish. When cool, fold in celery and beets. Turn into molds to set. Unmold on crisp lettuce. Serve topped with mayonnaise.

∘ — ∘ — ∘ — • — • — ∘ — ∘ — ∘ — ∘

Seasoned flour ⇆ To prepare

seasoned flour, add one to two teaspoons salt and one-quarter teaspoon pepper to each cup flour. Mix thoroughly.

Lime, Pepper, Salad

1 pkg. lime jello
1 cup boiling water
2 - 3 oz. pkgs. cream cheese
½ cup chopped pecans
2 large bell peppers
stuffed olives, sliced
pimientoes, sliced
paprika

Dissolve jello with boiling water. When beginning to set add cream cheese, creamed, nuts, olives, pimientoes, and paprika. Cut stems off peppers, clean, and soak one minute in boiling water. Cut top off peppers and fill with mixture. Put on ice, stand-up on ends. When hard and nearly ready to serve, slice length-wise with knife dipped in boiling water. Serve on lettuce and top with mayonnaise.

<u>Stuffed Artichokes</u>

6 artichokes
3 cups Seasoned Bread Crumbs
2 cups fresh parmesan cheese, grated
1 tsp. sweet basil
1 tbsp. parsley, minced
1 tsp. thyme
2 garlic cloves, minced
½ tsp. black pepper
½ tsp. salt
1 cup olive oil

Wash artichokes, cut off stems and trim tips of all leaves with scissors. Now open all leaves and rinse. Rub lemon around the outside of each 'choke. Mix all ingredients with the cheese, except the oil, to form a paste. Place this mixture by spoonfuls between the leaves. Pour the olive oil around all of the leaves. Place the artichokes in a deep pot with about 2 inches of hot water. Add ⅓ teaspoon salt and cover with tightly fitting lid. Be sure water does not boil over artichokes. Boil about 30 minutes or until artichokes are tender. *When a leaf pulls out easily it is done.*

Spinach Salad

Toss shredded, young, tender leaves of spinach (dry) with Vinaigrette dressing —*see below*. Top with sliced hard-boiled eggs.

Vinaigrette Dressing

To basic French dressing add 3 tablespoons tarragon vinegar, 1 tablespoon chopped pickles. 1 tablespoon chopped green olives and 1 tablespoon of chopped pimiento.

Maitre d'Hotel Sauce

¼ cup butter   ½ tsp. parsley, minced
½ tsp. salt   1 tbsp. lemon juice
⅛ tsp. pepper

Work butter until creamy. Add salt, pepper and parsley. Then add lemon juice very slowly. Spread over hot broiled fish or steak.

Jellied Tomato Salad

1 can tomato soup
1 3oz. package cream cheese, mashed
2 tbsp. gelatine —*soak in a little cold water*
¾ cup celery, chopped
¾ cup bell pepper, chopped
2 tbsp. onion, minced
½ cup mayonnaise
   salt to taste

Pour soup in a pot and add ¾ soup can of water. Heat until melted, then add gelatine to dissolve. Let cool and add mashed cheese and mayonnaise. Mix the vegetables together and add. Place in refrigerator to congeal. Serve on crisp, dry, lettuce. Serves from six to eight.

Cornucopia Salad

Roll thin slices of bologna, spiced or boiled ham, to form cornucopias. Fill with poato salad.

Cheese Biscuits

2 cups flour
3 tsp. baking powder
I cup sharp cheddar cheese, grated
I tsp. salt
4 tbsp. shortening
¾ cup milk

To flour, add baking powder, salt and sift. Cut in the shortening and the cheese with two knives, blending until the mixture resembles coarse corn meal. Add the milk slowly, stirring in with a fork to make a soft dough—*you may not need quite all the ¾ cup of milk*—or until flour leaves sides of bowl and follows fork. Continue stirring until all flour disappears. Turn out on lightly floured board and knead for about ½ minute. Turn smooth side up and pat or roll ½ inch thick. Cut with a floured biscuit cutter. Place biscuits on a greased baking sheet and bake at 450°F. 12 to 15 minutes. Makes 14 to 16 two inch biscuits.

Whipping Cream Biscuits

2 cups flour
3 tsp. baking powder
I cup heavy whipping cream
I tsp. salt

Add the baking powder and salt to the flour and sift.
Whip the cream and blend in with the flour lightly with a fork.
Now follow same proceedure as given for the cheese biscuits.

This recipe has been used along the Bayou for over one hundred years.

80

Garlic Bread

Slice a loaf of French Bread to about
1/4 inch of bottom, leaving enough
bread between slices to hold the
loaf together. Cream 1 stick butter
or oleo. Press 2 large garlic cloves
through a garlic press and add to
creamed butter, blending well.
Open each bread slice and spread
one side generously with garlic
butter. Place in 400°F. oven for
about ten minutes, or until well
heated through.
<u>For a variation</u>, after spreading garlic
butter on bread slices, sprinkle with
finely grated fresh pamesan cheese
and bake as directed above.

Party Cheese Straws

1 stick butter or oleo
2 cups sharp cheddar cheese —
1½ cups flour   grated
1 tsp. baking powder
½ tsp. salt
¼ tsp. pepper, red — or less

Cream the butter and add grated
cheese slowly. Cream together well
and then mix in all other ingredients.
Roll out to a thickness of 1/8 inch,
cut in strips ½ inch wide and bake
at 350°F. until delicately brown.
Keep "staws" in freezer. For guests remove
needed number and heat while preparing refreshments. Delicious, satisfying.

Banana - Nut Bread

1½ cups flour
2 tsp. baking powder
½ tsp. baking soda
½ tsp. salt
½ cup soft shortening
½ cup sugar
1 egg
1½ cups ripe bananas, mashed
1 cup whole bran cereal
1 tsp. vanilla
½ cup chopped nutmeats

To flour add baking powder, soda and salt. Blend shortening and sugar thoroughly and mix well, add egg and beat. Stir in banana, cereal and vanilla. Add this to flour mixture with nut meats, stirring only until combined. Spoon into greased loaf pan. Bake at 350°F. about one hour, or until a tooth pick inserted comes out clean. Remove from pan, cool.

For party use, fill six greased 6-ounce frozen-orange-juice cans about half way to the top. Bake at 350°F. about 30 minutes. Makes six round loaves.
Store overnight for easy slicing.

82

Southern Corn Bread

1 cup yellow cornmeal
1 tsp. salt
1 tbsp. shortening
2 eggs, well beaten
½ cup boiling water
2 tsp. baking powder
  milk as needed

Sift the cornmeal and salt, scald well with boiling water. Add shortening and beaten egg. Beat well, add enough milk, slowly, to make a soft batter, and add the baking powder while beating. Bake in a greased pan at 400°F. until brown.

Cinnamon Treats: Cream 2½ tbsp. butter, ⅓ cup sugar, ½ tsp cinnamon and ¼ tsp vanilla. Spread on thin bread slices, cut in strips or fancy shapes. Bake at 375°F until lightly brown.

Pain Perdu or, Lost Bread

4 slices of bread
1 egg
⅛ tsp. salt
1 tbsp. sugar
¼ cup milk
  a few drops of vanilla

Beat egg, add salt, sugar, milk and vanilla. Pour into shallow dish, dip bread into mixture and let it absorb as much as possible on both sides. Place slices in greased pan and put in 400°F. oven until dry and brown.

We often like to brown it in a pan on top of the stove in plenty of butter (olea).
Nice served with butter and honey, or dusted with powdered sugar.

84

for your personal notes and recipes

Equivalent Measurements: Dash = less than 1/8 tsp. ; 3 tsp. = 1 tbsp.
16 tbsp. = 1 cup;   2 cups = 1 pint
2 pints (4 cups) = 1 quart; 4 quarts = 1 gallon

Cookies + Cakes + Candies

Pecan Chewies

1 lb. light brown sugar
3 cups broken pecan pieces
1 tsp. vanilla
1½ cups flour
¼ tsp. salt
1 stick oleo
1 cup raisins
3 eggs
2 tsp. baking powder

Combine raisins and pecans and dredge in ½ cup flour. Cream butter and sugar, add eggs and vanilla. Combine one cup flour and baking powder, then sift into the wet mixture gradually, mixing well. Add pecans and raisins. Bake in square pan at 275° F. 45 min. or longer.

Fruit Cake Cookies

1 stick oleo
2 lbs. candied cherries
2 lbs. candied pineapple
2 lbs. raisins
2 tsp. soda
2 tbsp. milk
3 cups flour
2 cups, or more, broken pecans

4 eggs
1 cup whiskey
1½ cups dark brown sugar, packed
1 tsp. each of cinnamon, cloves, allspice and nutmeg

Cream oleo and sugar, add one egg at a time and beat well. Add whiskey and milk and beat. Sift dry ingredients and add. Sprinkle fruit with ½ cup flour, add fruit and nuts to mixture. Drop by spoonfuls on greased tin. Bake at 300° F. 15 to 20 minutes. (200 cookies.) Store in tin. Freeze perfectly.

Whiskey Balls or Rum

1 box vanilla wafers
2 tbsp. cocoa
1 cup confectioner's sugar
2 tbsp. karo – light color
3 jiggers whiskey or dark rum
2 cups chopped pecans

Roll wafers into fine crumbs add cocoa and sugar, mix. Mix the karo and whiskey and add to mixture. Then add the pecans and form balls about one-half inch in diameter. Roll balls well in confectioner's sugar. *Good!* and they keep well.

Apricot Balls

1 box (2 cups) dried apricots
1/2 cup confectioner's sugar – 1 cup nutmeats

Grind apricots and nutmeats together, fine. Work with fingers, shape into small balls. Roll in confectioner's sugar.

Butterscotch Slices

2 cups flour
1/2 tsp. soda
1 tsp. cream of tartar
1/2 tsp. salt
3 cups shortening
1 cup brown sugar
1 egg
1 tsp. vanilla
1/2 cup chopped pecans

Mix all ingredients thoroughly. Shape roll size desired for serving. Wrap in storage paper and chill in refrigerator. Slice one-eighth inch thick. Place on ungreased cooky sheet. Bake at 325°F. until done or a golden brown.

It's true! "Sugar and spice make everything nice." It is also known that sugar is an economical source of quick energy, quickly absorbed.

Pecan Tarts

for the cheese pastry ↪
    1 3-oz package cream cheese
    ½ cup butter or oleo
    1 cup all-purpose flour

        Let cream cheese and butter soften at room temperature; blend together. Stir in flour. Chill about one hour. Shape in twenty four (24) one-inch balls and place in ungreased 1-¾ inch muffin pans. Press dough against bottoms and sides.

for the pecan filling ↪
    1 egg
    ¾ cup brown sugar
    1 tbsp. butter or oleo
    1 tsp. vanilla
      dash salt
    ⅔ cup broken pecans

Beat together egg, brown sugar, butter, vanilla and salt just until smooth. Divide half the pecans among the pastry-lined pans. Add the egg mixture and top with remaining pecans. Bake at 325°F. for twenty-five minutes, or till filling is set. Cool; remove from pans.

Banana Drop Cookies

1½ cups sugar   2 tsp. baking powder
⅔ cup shortening   ¼ tsp. soda
1 tsp. vanilla   ½ tsp. salt
2 eggs   1 cup chopped nuts
2¼ cups all-purpose flour–1 tsp. cinnamon
1 cup crushed, ripe, bananas –about 3

Cream 1¼ cups sugar (reserve the rest)
shortening and vanilla until light
and fluffy. Add eggs and beat well.
Stir in the mashed bananas, flour,
baking powder, soda and salt. Mix
well. Stir in the nuts. Chill mixture
30 minutes in refrigerator. Drop
by teaspoonful on greased baking
sheet two inches apart. Mix the
sugar and cinnamon evenly and
sprinkle over the cookie dough.
Bake at 400°F. for 8 to 10 minutes,
or until a light brown. (about 5 dozen)

Butter Fingers

1 cup butter
5 tbsp. powdered sugar
2 cups flour
2 cups nuts, broken
1 tsp. vanilla

Work butter, sugar and flour
together in a bowl. Then add vanilla
and nuts, work-in. Form into
fingers and bake in slow oven,
300°F. until set, but not brown.
While warm roll in confectioner's
sugar.

Nut Kisses

1 cup broken nuts   1 cup confectioner's sugar
1 cup dates   2 egg whites
Beat egg whites stiff, stir in sugar, nuts and
dates. Drop by spoonfuls on cookie
sheet and bake <u>very</u> slowly till light brown.

Huguenot Torte

4 eggs
3 cups sugar
8 tbsp. flour
5 tsp. baking powder

½ tsp. salt
3 cups chopped tart cooking apples
2 cups chopped pecans or walnuts
2 tsp. vanilla

Beat whole eggs in electric mixer, or rotary beater, until very frothy and lemon colored. Add other ingredients in above order. Pour into two well-buttered baking pans about 8x12 inches. Bake in 325°F. oven about 45 minutes or until crusty and brown. To serve, scoop up with pancake turner, keeping crusty side on top. Pile on a large plate and cover with whipped cream and a sprinkling of the chopped nuts. You can also make sixteen (16) individual servings if you so desire.

Quaker Oats Oatmeal Cookies

3/4 cup shortening, soft	1 tsp. vanilla
1 cup firmly-packed brown sugar	1 cup all-purpose flour
1/2 cup white sugar	1 tsp. salt
1 egg	1/2 tsp. soda
1/4 cup water	3 cups Oats, uncooked

Beat shortening, sugars, egg, water and vanilla together until creamy. Sift together flour, salt and soda; add to creamed mixture; blend well. Stir in Oats. Drop by teaspoonfuls onto greased cookie sheets. Bake in pre-heated oven at 350°F. 12 to 15 minutes.

The above recipe appears on the current "Quick Quaker Oats" packages and is *so good* we are including it here. Men particularly enjoy these cookies. They remain fresh, when properly stored, a fairly long time. Several varieties can easily be made from the basic batter. Mixed as directed the recipe makes 5 dozen cookies. Part of the batter use for plain oatmeal cookies; add to remainder, raisins, chopped nuts or chocolate chips — easy!

Martha's Georgia Strawberry Shortcake

Take one level cup flour,
into it sift two level teaspoons
    baking powder (Calumet),
and one level teaspoon salt,
2 "egg size" daubs of Crisco,
1 egg
and 4 soup spoons water and
mix all with a fork or your hands.
Pat into a pan, forming in a round
shape, and bake at 375°F. until brown.
Slice in half to make two layers.
Butter both top and bottom layers.
Place prepared and sweetened
strawberries on bottom, cover
with top layer and top this with
strawberries and whipped cream.

Fudge Cake – lucie's own

1 stick butter
1 square bitter chocolate
2 eggs
1 cup sugar
2 cups pecans, broken
½ cup flour
  vanilla

Melt butter and chocolate in double
boiler. Beat eggs and add to the above,
when it cools. Mix the pecans with the
flour and add this to the mixture. Now
add about one teaspoon vanilla and stir
well. Place in 8 inch buttered square
pan and bake at 325°F. until a tooth
pick comes out clean, about 30 minutes.
Frost cake with one cup powdered
sugar mixed with three tablespoons
hot milk, 3 tbsp. cocoa and ½ tbsp. butter.
Mix well. Spread on cake and allow to dry.

Peanut Brittle

1½ cups sugar, white
1½ tsp. soda
2 cups shelled peanuts
   a piece of paraffin, thimble size
½ cup white Karo syrup
½ cup water

Put all ingredients in heavy boiler except the soda. Cook over a low fire, stirring constantly. When peanuts start popping, candy is done. Remove from fire, add soda, stir quickly and pour onto a buttered pan about 6 or 8 by 10 inches. Do NOT stir after pouring. Let cool thoroughly.

note:

   You will find several very good cake recipes in section titled "Favorites of Family and Friends."

a Quick and Tasty Cake

To one box of "Betty Crocker Yellow Cake Mix" add two teaspoons of instant coffee and two tablespoons of molasses. Prepare and bake as directed on package, only use a large pan to make one layer. To serve, cut in squares and top with whipped cream if desired.

This recipe was given us by caterers from San Antonio, Texas.

Mocha Butter Frosting

½ cup butter   salt, few grains
1 lb. powdered sugar   3 tbsp. strong, hot, coffee
3 tbsp. cocoa   1½ tbsp. vanilla

Cream butter, add sugar and cocoa slowly. stirring well till blended, add salt. Stir in coffee a little at a time to give a good spreading consistency and beat until fluffy.

Pineapple CAKE – leila's

1 cup butter
2 cups sugar
3 cups flour

3 tsps. baking powder
1 cup milk
4 eggs

Crushed pineapple, drained

Cream together thoroughly the butter and sugar. Add flour and baking powder (which have been sifted together) alternately with milk. Add one egg at a time, beating after each egg is added. Bake in three 9 inch pans or four 8 inch pans in 350°F. oven 25 to 30 minutes until lightly brown (cake tester comes out clean.) Put crushed pineapple between layers. Frost with creamy butter frosting or 7-minute frosting.

extra: CREAM CHEESE ICING – for any suitable cake.

1 3oz. package cream cheese
½ cup butter, soft
2 tbsps. cream
1 tbsp. lemon juice

3 tsps. lemon rind, grated
1 tsp. vanilla
4 cups confectioners' sugar, sifted

Combine and beat until light and fluffy.

Million Dollar Fudge

It's a lot of Fudge — 5 pounds and a half! But one often is wondering what to do for a fund raising sale, a church bazar, large children's party, et cetra.

4½ cups sugar
2 tbsp. butter or oleo
1 tall can evaporated milk
1 package, 12 ounces, semi-sweet chocolate bits
3 bars, 4 ounces each, German's sweet chocolate
1 jar marshmallow creme — 7 or 8 ounces
2 cups broken nut meats
pinch of salt

Stir together in a sauce pan the sugar, salt, butter and milk. Boil for 6 minutes. In a large bowl, place the chocolate bits, broken-up chocolate bars and the marshmallow creme. Pour the boiling syrup over these ingredients and beat or stir until chocolate is melted. Now stir in nuts and pour into a 12 x 8 x 2 inch buttered pan. Let stand a few hours before cutting in squares. Store in a tight container. 5½ pounds of delicious candy.

-by request. A special treat for a very particular Birthay or Anniversary.

BAKED ALASKA   —ice cream, sponge cake, meringue.

On a board covered with brown paper place a sheet of sponge cake one inch thick, cut a little larger than the ice cream.
Prepare the meringue; 3 egg whites ⏜ ⅛ tsp. cream of tartar ⏜ 1 tsp. vanilla ⏜ ½ cup of sugar. Beat egg whites with the cream of tartar and vanilla until stiff but not dry. Gradually beat in the sugar, sprinkling a little at a time over the surface of the egg whites. Continue beating until very smooth and glossy. Pre-heat oven and have it hot at 400°F.
Now place the ice cream on the sponge cake. Cover ice cream and sides of cake with meringue. Be _sure_ to cover _all_ the ice cream thoroughly. Bake in the hot oven until lightly browned, about five minutes. Serve at once.

for your personal notes and recipes

Time Table for Cooking Most Meats

Beef: Rare, 15 minutes per pound;
well done, about 20 minutes
Fowls: 20 minutes per pound on the average
Lamb: 30 minutes per pound
Pork: 30 minutes per pound
Veal: 30 minutes per pound

Equivalent Measurements

Dash = less than 1/8 tsp.
3 teaspoons = 1 tablespoon
16 tablespoons = 1 cup
2 cups = 1 pint
2 pints (4 cups) = 1 quart
4 quarts (liquid) = 1 gallon

Desserts and Beverages

Heavenly Japanese Mandarin Orange Dessert

Beat one egg in the top of a double boiler; stir in 3 tablespoons each of lemon juice and granulated sugar. Cook over hot water about five minutes or until thick, stirring constantly. Cool. Fold in ½ cup heavy cream, whipped, one 11-ounce can of Mandarin oranges, one cup miniature marshmallows, and one cup sliced bananas. Refrigerate overnight. Before serving, fold in ½ cup slivered toasted almonds. Spoon over slices of sponge cake. Very good served in parfait glasses accompanied by cookies.

Bananas on the Bayou

Peel bananas, one per person (or more!); split in half, lengthwise. Fry in butter or oleo, till brown. Serve hot on dessert plate. Top with whipped cream — or, sprinkle with brown sugar and lemon juice and dot with butter and broil 3 inches from heat until lightly browned. If you desire pour a little rum or sherry over bananas and bake. Depending on cooking method, serve as a vegetable or desert.

Delicious Melba

vanilla ice cream
peaches, brandied, fresh or canned.
currant jelly
apple jelly

The jellies are melted. Over each serving of ice cream place one peach half, cut side down, and pour melted jelly over all. (Plain peaches can be used)

To brandy peaches, take a good brand of canned peaches and drain off syrup. Combine an equal amount of syrup and cognac or whiskey and cover peach halves. Prepare at least a day before using.

Peaches Flambé

3 tbsp. sugar
3 tbsp. butter
3 peaches, halved (pears or pineapple can be substituted)
2 ounces cognac, dark rum or liquor

Caramelize sugar over low heat, add butter, stirring until dissolved. Cook over very low heat for 4 to 5 minutes. Add peaches and simmer until tender, basting occasionally. To be sure the liquor will flame when added, be sure the temperature of the fruit is above 75°F. (It is good to serve above fruit in a chaffing dish or electric skillet). Be sure to have the liquor warm, too. After pouring the liquor over the fruit, cover the pan before lighting; use a long taper; dim room lights.

Fruit Cup

tiny balls of fresh cantaloupe
red watermelon balls
strawberries whole and-or halved
raspberries
small, seedless grapes, halved
sliced fresh peaches
pear slices
or any other fruit

The addition of lemon or lime juice to each 'cup' usually improves the flavor. Garnish with sprigs of mint, a red cherry or a small dip of fruit ice or sherbet. To give color, grenadine syrup or green crème de menthe may be added, a little poured over each serving.

This is a good first course as well as a dessert, as listed here. If desired, add a good brandy to prepared fruit and store one hour in refrigerator.

bobie's Cream Tarts

Tart filling: ¾ cup sugar   2 cups milk
           ⅓ cup all purpose flour   3 egg yolks, slightly beaten
              <u>OR</u> 3 tbsp. corn starch   2 tbsp. butter
           ¼ tsp. salt   1 tsp. vanilla

<u>Tart shells</u>: use Betty Crocker Pie Dough;
prepare as directed on package.
Roll out dough about ⅛ inch thick
on floured board and cut out
rounds about 1½ inch wider than
diameter of tart pans. Fit each
round into tart pan, trim edges and
prick through pastry with tine of
fork. Bake as directed. Two sticks pie dough make 18 tarts.

<u>NOTE:</u> See next page for filling variations.

<u>Cream filling</u>: In saucepan combine sugar, flour, salt, and gradually stir in milk till mixture is smooth. Cook and stir over medium heat till mixture boils and thickens — then cook two minutes longer. Stir a small amount of the hot mix into the egg yolks and return to hot mixture. Cook two minutes, stirring constantly. Remove to room temperature. Add butter and vanilla, cover with plastic wrap; when cool pour into shells. Filling can be made a day ahead and kept in refrigerator.

<u>A Delicious Dessert</u> — pargie's

1 pound cake (about 50¢ size)
2 packages dark chocolate Royal Pudding
½ pint whipping cream

Into a large bowl break the pound cake in smallish pieces. Cook the pudding as directed on package. Take pudding from heat and pour over pieces of cake immediately, distributing well. Cover bowl tightly with wax paper and set aside to cool. Store overnight in refrigerator. When ready to serve, whip cream stiff and fold into the pudding and cake mixture, reserving a part for decorating top of each serving. Nice to serve in sherbert or parfait glasses.

<u>Tart filling variations</u>: Angel flake coconut may be folded into the cream filling to make delicious coconut cream tarts.
<u>For strawberry tarts</u> — put a little filling in each tart shell; arrange strawberries on top.
Whipped cream is often passed in a bowl.

WEDDING PUNCH

To one bottle of Sauterne wine add nine bottles of "7up". Pour over block of ice in punch bowl. To estimate requirements, figure five plus punch cups to a quart of liquid.

Spicy Sip Tropical Cooler

1 cup chilled lime juice
2 cups pineapple juice
1 quart carbonated water
⅛ tsp. ginger

⅛ tsp. allspice
⅛ tsp. cloves
1¼ cups sugar
2 egg whites

Have juices and carbonated water well chilled. Mix spices with sugar. Beat egg whites until frothy, carefully add sugar mixture, and beat until mix forms peaks. Fold into mixed liquids and serve at once in tall glasses. Serves eight.

CRÊPES SUZETTE

<u>Crêpes</u>: ½ cup flour, ½ teaspoon salt, 2 eggs, well beaten, ⅔ cup milk, 1 tablespoon crisco, melted

Sift flour, measure, add salt and sift again; add egg, milk and shortening in mixing bowl and beat until smooth. Pour enough batter onto a hot greased griddle to make ONE pancake about 4 to 5 inches in diameter. Tip pan to make the pancake as <u>thin</u> as possible. Bake until browned, turning to brown on both sides. Keep hot until all cakes are baked. Now spread with jelly (currant, or other tart jelly); roll; sprinkle with sugar if desired. Makes 10 to 12 pancakes.

Now for a special occasion, prepare a Suzette Sauce and serve the flaming dish with appreciative exclamations from your guests.

<u>Suzette Sauce</u>: ½ cup butter; ¼ cup sugar; 1 tbsp. orange rind, grated; ⅓ cup orange juice; 1 tsp. lemon rind, grated; ¼ cup Curaçao; Brandy <u>or</u> Grand Marnier, ½ cup. Melt butter over VERY low heat, using Crêpes Suzette cooker or a chafing dish. Gradually add sugar stirring well until blended. Add orange juice and rinds. Cook over low heat about 5 minutes or until slightly thickened. Now add Curaçao and mix well. Dip hot pancakes in sauce, roll or fold. Carefully place the rolled or folded pancakes in the Suzette sauce and heat about 1 minute, basting with sauce. Pour brandy or Grand Marnier over pancakes in sauce. Ignite and shake pan so whole pan flames. Serve on hot plates.

Peggy's Hot Spiced Cider

¾ cup light brown sugar
¼ tsp. salt
1 tsp. ground cloves
1 tsp. allspice
1½ tsp. cinnamon
½ tsp. nutmeg
2 quarts sweet cider

Thoroughly mix all ingredients except the cider. Then add to the cider in a saucepan and simmer ten minutes. Strain through double thickness of cheesecloth wrung out of hot water. Reheat punch and serve steaming.

Mint Punch — from the Colonel's Lady

Fresh mint
4 cups tea
½ cup sugar
2 oranges, juice
2 lemons, juice
2 bottles ginger ale

Pour hot tea over crushed mint. Add sugar, orange and lemon juice; cool. Just before serving pour in the gingerale and add ice. About 3 quarts. Garnish with slices of orange, lemon and whole sprigs of mint.
For about 200 cups of punch:
fresh mint (lots)   22 oranges, juice
45 cups tea   22 lemons, juice
5½ cups sugar   23 qts. ginger ale
Garnish as above. Served at a large Army Post reception. WW II.

Café Brûlot

1 cup Cognac — 40 small cubes sugar — 40 whole cloves
2 sticks cinnamon broken into small bits
½ orange, peeled, cut thin and broken into small bits
½ lemon, peeled, cut thin and broken into small bits
1 quart hot, dripped coffee

Shortly before serving, combine all ingredients, with the exception of coffee. When ready to serve, pour into Brûlot bowl. In Brûlot tray, put small amount of alcohol and light. Catch flame with ladle and hold over bowl. Result, a beautiful blue flame. To this, gradually add hot dripped coffee, continuously stirring. Pour in Brûlot cups and serve. (Another way to light the bowl is to fill a tablespoon with brandy, heat over a flame, light with match, ignite bowl)

French Drip Coffee

Every old home in the "sugar country" has a pot of this coffee resting in a pan of water; hot, or ready to heat, near the back of the stove. Each day is started with a demitasse of café noir — and throughout the day this coffee is brewed and enjoyed. Dark roast or chicory flavored coffee, drip grind, is always used. Take a French or drip pot and fill the section to the first ring. Moisten the dry coffee with cold water. Have the water kettle boiling and add only boiling water, gradually, a few tablespoons at a time. Allow the first boiling water plenty of time to drip through, then add as other water drips. A pinch of salt added to dry coffee grounds improves the taste. Keep coffee hot by setting pot in a pan of hot water on stove.

Café au lait is favored by many and is often a change from café noir. It is made by pouring, at the same time, hot milk and hot coffee, filling the cup with a 50/50 mixture.

OLD SLAVE EGGNOG

Some years ago a visitor, from an old New Orleans family, to the lovely ante-bellum home where we lived, sent us this recipe. The first sentence of his letter was, "Old Slave Eggnog is not just another recipe. It is a HERITAGE that has been handed down from generation to generation." To the best of our information, the only previous publication was in my wife's book "Oaklawn Manor," published in 1966. Mr. Bernard Bares' recipe follows. Separate the yolks and whites from 12 eggs and place in separate bowls. Place the yolks in a very large bowl where all ingredients will be placed. Add 1 cup cane sugar to yolks and beat well. Now add 1 quart half/half milk and cream and 4 tbsp. of vanilla and beat well. Then stir in 6 ounces any good quality light rum, do not use dark rum, and 1 pint any good whiskey and let batter stand. Beat the whites of eggs adding ½ cup powdered sugar and 1 tbsp. vanilla. Beat until stiff. In a separate bowl whip 1 pint of whipping cream and slowly add ½ cup powdered sugar and 1 tbsp vanilla. Beat well to whipped cream consistency. Place the whipped cream and the whites of eggs into the original yolk batter and beat thoroughly. Add 2 quarts of milk and beat until foamy. Place in refrigerator and let stand for several hours before serving. If desired, a dash of nutmeg per cup.

<u>Ingredients for ½ recipe:</u> 6 eggs   2 tbsp. vanilla   ½ pt. whipping cream
1 cup cane sugar 3 oz. light rum   ¼ cup powdered sugar
1 pt. ½-½ cream/milk - ½ pt. whiskey   1 tsp. vanilla
1 qt. milk

for your personal notes and recipes

Special ↩   Sparkling <u>Catawba</u> grape juice, <u>cold</u>,
in champagne glasses. Serve when a
non alcoholic cocktail is desired. It is
attractive and delicious.   ◇   ◇   ◇ Mr. Gee.

"Catawba" ↩ a light, red, variety of
                American grape.

Favorites — of Family and Friends

These recipes are mostly from Lousiana,

bobie's Braunschweiger Glacé

2 tbsp. unflavored gelatine (1 envelope)
½ cup cold water   3 tbsp. mayonnaise
1 can condensed consommé   1 tbsp. vinegar
½ lb. roll braunschweiger 1 tbsp. minced onion

Soften gelatine in cold water. Heat consommé to boiling. Remove from heat; add gelatine and stir until dissolved. Pour into a 2 cup mold. Chill till firm. Blend remaining ingredients. Spoon out center of jellied consommé leaving ½ inch on all sides. Fill center with meat mixture. Heat spooned out consommé till melted, pour over braunschweiger. Chill firm and unmold. Trim with slices of hard-boiled eggs or olives, halved. Serve with slices of "party rye".

tom 3rd's Baked Pork Chops

4 loin pork chops (about 1 pound)
1 tbsp. butter
1 can cream of celery soup
⅓ cup evaporated milk
1½ tsp. "Kitchen Bouquet"
1 small onion, thinly sliced
salt and pepper

Lightly salt and pepper chops and brown on both sides in oven proof skillet. Remove chops and sauté onion in butter until just tender. Pour off drippings, stir in soup, milk and Kitchen Bouquet. Return chops to pan, cover and bake in 350°F. oven for 1 hour.

miss elizabeth's <u>Broiled Chicken</u>

A chicken weighing 2 pounds, or less. (have butcher cut in half)
Salt and pepper chicken the night before; store in refrigerator.
Cut up giblets and fry in a heavy pot in oleo until brown.
Add water or chicken broth and make extra gravy to be used with chicken.

Melt ½ stick oleo, or more, in a long baking pan. Dot chicken all over with
oleo; place ½ slice onion in pan and place chicken half breast down,
a slice for each breast. Place strips of celery on top of chicken.

Place under broiler flame. Baste often with juice. When chicken gets
a light brown, turn over and cook until same on other side, basting.
Turn again and pour "extra gravy" over chicken. When done (test with a
fork) leave breast down in pan gravy to keep 'till serving. If heated
later, cover with foil.

peggy's Chicken Strata

8 slices day old white bread
2 cups cooked chicken, diced
½ cup onion, chopped
½ cup bell pepper, chopped
½ cup celery, finely chopped
½ cup mayonnaise

¾ tsp. salt — dash of pepper
2 eggs, slightly beaten
1½ cup milk
1 can cream of mushroom soup
½ cup shredded cheese

Butter 2 slices of bread, cut into ½ inch cubes and set aside. Cut remaining bread slices into 1 inch cubes. Place ½ unbuttered cubes in bottom of an 8"x 8"x 2" baking dish. Combine chicken, vegetables, mayonnaise and seasonings then spoon ½ of the combination over bread cubes, sprinkle with cheese and cover with rest of unbuttered cubes. Now spoon over rest of chicken mixture and sprinkle with remaining cheese. Pour over the above the combined eggs milk and soup. Place buttered cubes on top. Cover and chill one hour. Now bake at 325°F. for 50 minutes. serves six.

tom 3rd's Barbecue Sauce (not for chicken, see page)

In a heavy saucepan melt ½ lb. oleo and add 4 large onions, diced, 3 garlic cloves, diced, and cook until tender. Then add 1 cup water, ¼ cup dark molasses and ½ bottle worcester sauce, 1 tbsp. (or more) liquid smoke, 4 tbsp. creole mustard and ½ btl. catsup. Stir and simmer 30-45 min. Add water if needed; cook until ingredients blend.

bobie's _Pickled Okra_

2 cups vinegar, ¼ cup water, 2 tbsp. salt,
hot peppers, garlic cloves, fresh okra
Sterilize jars and lids, qt. jars. Wash
okra well and cut off stems. Combine
vinegar, water and salt in saucepan and
simmer; keep simmering while using. Pack
raw, clean, okra in hot, clean qt. jars, placing
pointed ends down in first layer. Place 2
garlic cloves and a strip of fresh hot
pepper over okra and pack tight; add
another layer of okra and fill jar ¼
from top with simmering solution.

<u>Hint</u>: <u>To chop or mince an onion</u>
Peel onion and cut in half from stem to
other end. Lay cut side on board
and slice from end to end, leaving
small amount at top end. Vary thickness
of slices for fine or coarse chopped
pieces. Now cut <u>across</u> slices from
end to end.

bobie's _Marinated Shrimp_

sliced onions   ½ cup vinegar
bay leaves   2 tsp. salt
1 tsp. dry mustard 3 tsp. celery salt
1 cup salad oil   10 dashes pepper sauce
3 pounds shrimp, cleaned and cooked
Mix ingredients well, omitting shrimp.
Alternate layers of shrimp with white
onions and bay leaf, use a rectangular
bake dish. Pour mixture over shrimp
24 hours before serving - refrigerate.
Serve as appetizer or on lettuce as salad.

mme. benguet's _Personal Cheese Spread_ "2d hand" from a friend

½ pound Roquefort cheese, small bits
4 pkgs. (8 oz) cream cheese, (vary to taste)
8 large green olives, sliced thin
6 large shallots, chopped fine
1 medium dill pickle, minced
Combine all, refrigerate.

babe's <u>Estouffade de Boeuf à la Niçoise</u>

Have your butcher cut a 2 inch pot roast and de-bone.
In a heavy saucepan brown both sides, cover roast with fresh sliced tomatoes.
Add ½ pint white or red wine, 12 stoned black olives and bouquet garni (rosemary and bay leaf).
Cook slowly over fairly low fire until meat is tender.

lucie's <u>Interesting Chile Dish</u>

This entails making individual servings by placing layers of different ingredients on a plate and topping them with very hot chili. (Chili hot from the fire to melt the cheese).
Into a plate put a layer of Fritos.
Then a layer of onions, finely chopped —
then a layer of cabbage, chopped small —
finally, a layer of sharp cheese, (sharp cheddar is very good).

Pour over all a layer of hot, hot, chili (without beans) and serve immediately. (Hot heat, not taste!)

bob's Meat Balls with Noodles

5 pounds ground meat
1½ cups seasoned Italian Bread crumbs
1 tbsp. soy sauce
2 eggs
½ can evaporated milk
1 tbsp. grated onion
salt and pepper to taste

Combine all ingredients thoroughly and form by teaspoonfuls into balls. Bake at 350°F. until brown.
(makes 100 meat balls)
Prepare following to serve with meat balls *over* noodles or rice:
6 cans Franco-American Beef gravy
½ pint sour cream
Heat the gravy and cream together, add meat balls (hot) and serve over the noodles or rice.

joanie's Stuffed Flounder Casserole

1 pkg. frozen flounder fillets, (thawed)
2 cups dried bread cubes
½ cup celery, chopped
¼ cup onion, chopped
1 cup cooked shrimp, chopped
evaporated milk
1 can frozen cream of shrimp soup (thawed)
salt, pepper, paprika
Place half of fillets in buttered casserole dish. Combine bread cubes, celery, onion and shrimp; add salt, pepper and paprika to taste and moisten with milk. Spread this dressing over fillets and cover with remaining fillets, then spoon on shrimp soup. Cover and bake in 350°F. oven for 1 hour.
Serves four. (In place of frozen shrimp soup you can substitute, adding boiled shrimp & liquor to mushroom soup.)

emilie and billie's # *Chocolate Cheesecake*

<u>to form shell:</u>

1½ cups vanilla cookies, crushed

¼ cup melted butter

Put cookie crumbs in bowl and slowly stir-in melted butter. Press the mixture on the bottom and sides of a well-buttered 9 inch spring-form pan. Chill.

<u>for filling:</u>

4 egg yolks

4 egg whites

⅔ cup sugar

12 oz. semisweet chocolate

½ cup strong coffee

1 tsp. vanilla

salt, a dash

2 8-oz. packages cream cheese

Beat 4 egg yolks with ⅓ cup sugar until they are thick and lemon colored. In the top of a double boiler, over hot water, melt the semisweet chocolate and stir in coffee, vanilla and dash of salt. Beat in softened cream cheese and beat until mixture is smooth; let cool for 5 min. Slowly add chocolate-cheese mixture to egg yolks. Beat the egg whites with ⅓ cup sugar until they are stiff but not dry, fold them into the batter and pour filling into the chilled shell. Bake the cheesecake in a 350°F. oven for one hour, or until it is set. Turn off heat, open oven door and let the cheesecake cool in oven. Remove the pan sides and cover cheesecake with ½ cup whipped cream with 2 tbsp. sugar added. Garnish top with chocolate curls.

116

carole's **Page Boy Cookies**

2½ cups sugar
1 cup butter
2 eggs
½ cup Steen's Cane Syrup
1 tsp. soda
4½ cups all-purpose flour
½ tsp. salt
2 tsp. vanilla
1 cup nuts (optional)
(Dissolve soda in 4 tbsp. hot water and
sift salt with flour.)
Mix in order as listed in large bowl.
Form in a roll and chill overnight.
Slice in cookie thickness and place on
cookie sheet, baking about 10 minutes
at 325°F.

This makes a very crisp cookie
and if stored in a tight, closed,
container will remain crip for several
weeks. Dough may be frozen.

emmadell's **Pecan Pralines**

2 cups white sugar
1 cup dark brown sugar
1 stick oleo
5 cups pecans
3 tbsp. corn syrup
¼ cup milk

Combine all ingredients - *less pecans* - in
saucepan and cook until mixture forms
a soft ball in water. Remove from heat
and beat hard by hand until it leaves
side of pan. *It makes-up fast, so don't
delay beating.* Add pecans at the last
minute. Drop by tablespoonfuls on wax
paper, or, as we often do down here, drop
on a marble slab.

SOUR CREAM CAKE for Bundt Pan

NORMA CARROL MOORE, McComb, Miss.

2 sticks butter or oleo
2 cups sugar
3 eggs
2 tsp. vanilla

2¼ cups cake flour
½ tsp. salt
1 - tsp. baking powder
1 - carton sour cream

Cream butter and sugar thoroughly, add eggs one at a time, fold in sour cream alternately with flour that has been sifted with salt and baking powder; then add vanilla. Put half of this mixture in greased and lightly floured Bundt pan. Mix together ¾ cups chopped pecans, 2 tsps. sugar and 1 tsp. cinnamon. Sprinkle this evenly over batter that is in pan. Drizzle over this 2 tbsp. melted butter. Carefully add remaining batter on top. Bake at 325°F about one hour and fifteen minutes. Remove cake from oven and while still warm mix 1⅓ cups confectioners' sugar, 2 tbsps. milk, 1 tsp. vanilla. Use spoon to put on top of cake and let it drizzle down sides.
note: If you don't have a Bundt pan, get one. It has other uses, too.

grace's Viennese Coffee

Prepare strong coffee, (dripped coffee is best), cool.
For serving, place chocolate ice cream in tall glass and pour cold coffee over.

miss mimi's Orange Cake

1 cup sugar	1 tsp. salt
½ cup butter	½ cup nut meats
2 eggs	1 cup raisins
2 cups flour	1 orange rind, grated
1 cup buttermilk	1 tsp. vanilla
1 tsp. soda	

Cream butter and add sugar gradually until light and fluffy. Add eggs and beat thoroughly with electric mixer. Add vanilla, grated orange rind, nuts and raisins. Sift flour, soda and salt in separate dish. Now add dry ingredients alternately with buttermilk, hand stirring only enough after each addition to blend thoroughly. Do not beat. Pour into greased 8-or-9 inch pans and bake at 350°F. for about 30 to 35 minutes, or until done. Icing: 1 cup powdered sugar; ⅓ c. orange juice Mix and spread on cake while cake is still hot. It melts to make a thin icing (glaze). Use part melted butter with juice for richness

olga's Sad Cake Ice Cream

2 cups brown sugar	⅔ cup flour
2 eggs	1 cup nuts, broken
1 tsp. soda	2 tsp. vanilla

Cream sugar and eggs; add flour and soda, then nut meats and vanilla. Bake in moderate oven till cake tester comes out clean. Keep overnight and next day crumble, add one pint whipped cream and freeze.

mary beth's Lemon Sponge Cake

1 cup sugar	1 lemon, grated rind
2 tbsp. butter	5 tbsp. lemon juice
4 tbsp. flour	¼ tsp. salt

3 eggs, separate whites—1½ cup milk
Beat egg whites and yolks separately; cream butter and sugar. Add flour, lemon juice and rind, salt, egg yolks and milk. Mix well and fold in well beaten egg whites. Bake 45 minutes in greased custard cups set in pan of hot water. Bake at 325°F.

lucie's ----- DATE TORTE

1 pound pitted dates — 1 cup sugar — — 1cup water — 1 tbsp. lemon juice
Place water, dates and sugar in sauce pan and cook until soft, about five minutes.
Cool and add lemon juice.

1 cup brown sugar — 3/4 cup butter - 1½ cup flour - 1 tsp. soda - ½ tsp. salt -
1½ cup oatmeal
Sift flour, soda and salt in bowl, add brown sugar and butter, then mix
until crumbly. Gradually add the dry oatmeal.
Put one-half of mixture in a shallow, greased pan (10"x14") and pat into place
like pastry. Then spread the date mixture over this followed by the rest of the
dry mix on top.
Bake in a slow oven (325°F.) about 35 minutes. Increase the heat during the
last few minutes to brown top slightly.
Cut in bars or squares while warm.

pargie's — BISQUIT TORTONI

4 egg yolks; ½ cup sherry; 2/3 cup sugar (cook in double boiler until thick; set aside);
1 pt. whipping cream; 1 tsp. vanilla; ½ cup unsalted, toasted, chopped almonds; mix.
Fold cream mixture into custard, put into fluted paper muffin cups and sprinkle with about
6 crushed almond macaroons (day old ones crush more easily). This dessert can be
prepared well ahead. Stores well in deep freeze. (Delicious - the author.)

grace's <u>LEMON BARS</u>

            2 cups flour
            1 cup margarine (or butter)
            ½ cup powder sugar

Mix well – press into a flat pan (jelly roll size). Bake 20 minutes at 350°F.
While baking, mix :   4 eggs, well beaten
            2 cups sugar, continue beating
            1 tbsp. flour
            1 tsp. baking powder

Into the above, mix well, juice and grated rind of one lemon. Pour over first mixture
and bake another 20 minutes.

ellie's Apricot Nectar Cake

1 pkg. Duncan Hines "Lemon Supreme Cake Mix;" ½ cup Crisco oil; 1 cup apricot
nectar; juice of ½ lemon; ½ cup sugar. Mix all these together. Add 4 eggs,
one at a time, beating each egg well into mixture; pour smooth mixture into
a well greased tube pan. Bake at 325°F. for one hour. Cool for over an hour
before turning cake out of pan .

<u>For the Glaze</u>: In a small bowl put the juice from one large
lemon, add powdered sugar gradually, mixing with a teaspoon to icing
consistency. Glaze top and sides of cake. Glazed cake keeps moist very
well, stored in a covered cake container. (Thanks, Ellie, we have this <u>very</u> often).

Lurline's **CRISPY COOKIES**

1 cup soft oleo or butter   1½ cup granulated sugar
1 tsp. vanilla extract   2 large eggs (⅓ to ½ cup)

Beat until well mixed. Then sift together into mixture:

3 cups sifted flour   2 tsp. baking powder   1½ tsp. salt

Blend into stiff dough. Now, with an ice tea spoon, drop about half a spoonful on <u>ungreased</u> cooky pan and flatten with ½ of a small pecan. Place about an inch apart; bake for 8 to 10 minutes in preheated moderately hot oven, 375°F. Remove from pan immediately, <u>before cooling</u> - otherwise they break-up. Spread to cool on brown paper, store in tight container, or freeze. *The dough may be refrigerated in rolls, for a week or more and cookies baked as needed after slicing.* These cookies may be decorated with colored sugar, chopped or candied fruit, or as you desire.

Almond Crisps – Lurline

Prepare above ingredients, <u>adding</u> 1 tsp. almond flavoring *with the* vanilla. Sprinkle tops with granulated sugar and slivered almonds.

Irish Trifle

Line the bottom of a large bowl with fine sponge cake made about one inch thick. Spread with strawberry jam, currant jelly or your own favorite. Cover this merry dish with another layer of identical cake. Spread this, again, with jam and continue until a few inches below the top of the bowl. Now, pour in enough sherry to saturate the cake. Pour over it a good boiled custard (see below). Put bowl in refrigerator for ½ hour. Serve on large dessert plates surrounded by sliced up fruits – ripe and lightly sugared (peaches, apricots, pears, seedless grapes, sliced oranges, et cetra.) Serve large portions to the delighted guests. Now for the boiled custard: beat four egg yolks until pale yellow; mix in 3 tbsp. sugar; beat well again. Bring 3¼ cups of milk to a boil, pour over yolks. When well mixed put into a double boiler and cook until thickened, stirring constantly; then add 1 tbsp. vanilla.

Lurline says "these are light, _thin_ and tender-delicious." **BUTTERMILK PANCAKES**
2 eggs \ 1 cup buttermilk \ ⅓ cup flour \ ¼ tsp. salt. Shake or blend all together in a jar or plastic container. Drop batter on a hot greased griddle to make pancakes desired size, turn once when browned and keep hot until served. Serve with cottage cheese, berries, jams or your favorite syrup. (Try for crêpes suzette).

from our _Granddaughters_

nancy's _Prize Winning Pralines_*

½ cup pecan halves   1 cup brown sugar   ⅔ cup cane sugar   pinch salt

2 tbsp. butter   milk, to moisten   ½ tsp. vanilla

"Combine sugar, salt, pecans, butter. Gradually add enough milk to moisten; all in a heavy pot. Cook over low heat stirring constantly until mixture comes to a boil. Continue cooking to soft ball stage. Remove from fire, add vanilla and beat well. Drop on waxed paper by spoonfuls. Try to get the same amount of nuts in each one."   * St. Tammany Parish Fair

susan holmes potter's _Yams a la Haiti_

4 large yams   ½ stick melted butter   ¼ tsp. nutmeg

½ cup brown sugar   rind of 1 grated orange and lemon   ½ tsp. cinnamon

                           ¼ cup heated rum

"Boil yams. Peel and cut into ¼ inch slices. Grease casserole dish. Sprinkle ⅓ rd. of brown sugar into bottom of dish and moisten with ⅓ rd. of butter. Layer yam slices, brown sugar, orange and lemon rind, spices and butter. Top layers with hot rum and ignite at sideboard or dining table."

julie's **Pound Cake**

2 sticks butter   2 cups flour   2 cups sugar
5 large eggs   1 tsp. vanilla

Cream butter and sugar together thoroughly. Add flour, aternately with eggs, then add vanilla, mixing well, with electric beater.
Line bottom of cake pan with greased brown paper. Bake at 350°F. 30 minutes the test with cake tester. When done, tester comes out clean.

pamela lucile's **Brownies**

½ cup butter or oleo   1 cup brown sugar
2 squares Baker's Unsweetened   1 cup flour
    Chocolate   1 tsp. baking powder
2 tbsp. water   1 tsp. vanilla
2 eggs   1 cup broken pecans

Cream butter and sugar. Put water and chocolate in a sauce pan; over a slow fire melt the chocolate. Combine creamed butter-sugar with the melted chocolate. Beat the eggs and add to the above. Sift flour with baking powder, add nutmeats and combine with mixture. Butter a 10 inch square pan well, dust with flour and bake in a slow oven, 300° to 325°F. about 25 minutes. Let cool in pan awhile before cutting in squares.

---

roberta de voe's BEEF STROGANOFF

1 pound cooked beef steak or roast
 butter
1 onion, chopped
½ tsp. salt

1 tsp. celery seed
1 4-oz. can mushrooms
½ tsp. basil
½ cup sour cream

Cut meat into narrow strips. Melt butter over low heat and brown meat slightly. Add onions and cook until they are tender. Now add salt, celery seed, mushrooms basil and sour cream. Simmer 30 minutes and serve with noodles.

raised cottage

plantation dinner bell

buggy

shrimp lugger with net

passenger stern wheeler

For The Bride

a new section by:

Lucie

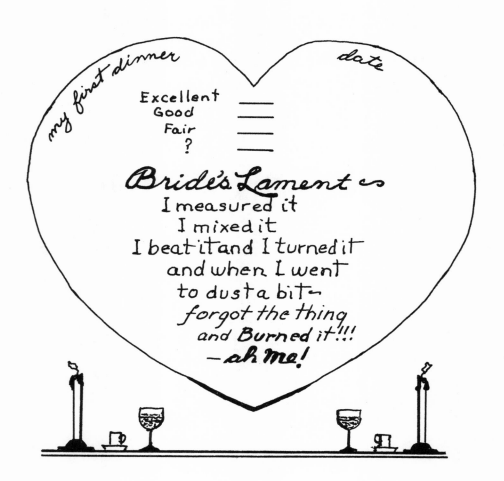

my first dinner   date

Excellent ___
Good ___
Fair ___
? ___

Bride's Lament

I measured it
I mixed it
I beat it and I turned it
and when I went
to dust a bit—
forgot the thing
and Burned it!!!
—ah me!

The Bride — Bless Her!

Here's to the wings of your Love
May they never lose a feather
While His Big Boots and
Your Little Shoes
Stand under the Bed Together!   *(old Swiss Toast)*

The Magic of Keeping
Your good man Happy — —
Good food, good Style —
Feed Him Well, with tender care, Then —
Be as Thoughtful of Him,
As polite to Him,
As true to Him as you'd be to
Your very Dearest Friend.

(Advice to our Five Granddaughter Brides)

Dear Bride: if you will master a few really good recipes, you can become famous as a "good cook". I found, to my surprise, when we lived on our first Army Post, that because I served my own Ice Box Rolls, or a Lemon Mousse as dessert, after a stuffed crab supper, my reputation as a good cook was established.

——————— a menu for a STUFFED CRAB supper ———————

Before sitting serve hot Bouillon, or broth, in mugs, or chilled Catawba grape juice (page 108) in wine size glasses. On a dinner plate place one hot stuffed crab, a lettuce leaf with six or more nice size shrimp, boiled and chilled, a tomato wedge and ½ boiled egg, a serving of green beans almondine (we use Del Monte French Style beans). Have a bowl of thousand island type dressing to pass and hot buttered rolls or garlic bread. For dessert, DeVoe's Lemon Mousse (page 69). Follow with after dinner coffee (page 106).

ICE BOX ROLLS ～ 1 cup boiling water, ⅓ cup sugar, 1½ tsp. salt, ¼ cup shortening, 4 cups sifted flour, 1 egg, 1 yeast cake, ⅛ cup warm water, ½ tsp. sugar. Mix first four ingredients, cool to luke warm. Dissolve yeast in warm water with ½ tsp. sugar. Combine this with above in a large bowl. Add egg and mix well. Add flour, 2 cups at a time, beat well. Cover tight and refrigerate for 24 hours. Roll dough on floured board, ½ inch thick. Cut with biscuit cutter dipped in butter, fold over. Let rise 4 hours in a warm place. Bake at 400°, 15-20 minutes.

Stuffed Crabs

1 lb. crab meat
6 slices stale bread, toasted
1 clove garlic, minced
1 medium size onion
½ green pepper
¼ cup cooking oil
Bread crumbs
Parsley, onion tops, celery tops, mince
Red pepper and salt to taste

Grind in meat grinder, bread, onions garlic, sweet pepper. Mix with crab meat, season. Put this into heated cooking oil. Keep flame moderate, stir well for twenty minutes. Add parsley, onion tops and celery. Fill well washed crab shells with this mixture, sprinkle tops with bread crumbs, large dot of butter put in 375 oven until crumbs are brown. Serves four, or more.

IMPERIAL CRAB

1 lb. crab meat
1 tsp. dry mustard
½ tsp. salt
½ cup mayonnaise
1 tbsp. capers
White pepper and paprika to taste and a dash of worchertershire

Pick over crab meat, leaving in as large pieces as possible. Blend mustard, salt and Worchestershire sauce, stir in mayonnaise and capers. Gently fold mixture in crab meat. Spoon into individual casseroles. Spread with light coating of mayonnaise. Sprinkle with paprika. Bake at 375° about 20 minutes or until top is golden brown. Serves four.

Cocktail party fun - <u>SHRIMP DIP</u>

1 6oz. pkg. Philadelphia Cream Cheese
1 cup boiled shrimp, ground
2 tbsps. finely chopped onions
Milk
Salt and pepper to taste
      Mix cream cheese with a little milk to a soft dip stage.
Then add mashed shrimp, onions, salt and pepper. Mix very
thoroughly. (Lucie says she has used 2 cans of whole shrimp-
(4½ oz size) - chopped fine and it is delicious. Follow directions on
can for rinsing shrimp.) This was also served with Fritos at a tea.

———

<u>Sausage Balls</u> - "Chick Snowden"

1 lb. Hot sausage (Tennessee Pride if possible)
1 stick Kraft's "Coon Cheese", or Pepper cheese, or sharp cheddar
3½ cups Bisquick.   Now, grate cheese while cold, mix with sausage
thoroughly. Slowly add sifted Bisquick and mix. Roll into bite size balls,
place on flat pan in 350° oven for about 25 to 30 minutes. These are
fine to prepare and wrap in foil and freeze. When ready to use,
place <u>unfrozen</u> in pan and cook as shown.

OYSTERS REINE

from "Bobie"

1 can mushroom soup, undiluted ～ 2 8oz. cans oysters, well drained and chopped ～ 1/4 cup green onions, minced ～ 1/4 cup chopped parsley ～ dash red pepper

Combine ingredients and heat slowly in a heavy pot. Do not allow to come to a boil. This will fill 24 small patty shells or 48 miniatures. Or serve in small dinner rolls which been hollowed out and toasted. (Good friends say that they think it tastes even better as a cold left-over.)

Catfish Squares

1½ to 2 lbs. catfish fillets cut in individual serving pieces about 1½ inch square (bite size). Roll in flour seasoned with salt and pepper. Fry in hot oil from 6 to 8 minutes. Drain and serve hot with tooth picks and a fish sauce if desired.

Remember ～ you don't have to serve alcoholic beverages; pass mugs of hot bouillon, no crackers, before lunch or dinner — men like this; (beef is good). Or, serve Welch's Red Grape Juice, chilled, in wine size glasses. To be different, serve cold Sparkling Catawba Grape Juice ～ see page 108.

Served at an informal plantation luncheon → → → →
Margaret's Creole Shrimp Casserole, a salad of grape fruit sections
and Avocado slices on lettuce, with French dressing. Let the
dessert be your favorite cake with demitasse coffee. Prepare
the shrimp casserole, as follows ∽
1½ cups raw rice; 1 can consomme; 1 can onion soup; 2 lbs raw, cleaned,
shrimp; 1 stick oleo, melted; now, mix all ingredients, put in casserole
(covered), bake at 350° one and one-half hours.

— and at a luncheon served in Hinsdale, Illinois, I enjoyed
this; a cranberry juice cocktail and served on a plate, half an
English muffin, a ham slice on top and toasted with mushroom sauce
poured over all. Also on plate, several long wedges of melons in season
(cantaloupe & honeydew), hot buttered rolls and for dessert, a scoop
of vanilla ice cream with butterscotch sauce. If you find a luncheon
menu that's simple to prepare, don't worry about repeating it.

This a quick, tasty sandwich, nice to serve:
   Toast with layers of sliced avocado,
      tomato, bacon and cheese, heated,
         and a favorite beverage. [use crisp bacon]

Chicken Loaf with Mushroom Sauce (serves 8-10)

14 lb. chicken, 1 cup cooked rice, 4 well beaten eggs
2 cups bread crumbs, 1½ tsp. salt, chicken stock

Stew chicken. Remove meat from bones and dice. Combine all ingredients and pour into an oiled 10 inch pan. Set in pan of hot water and bake uncovered in a 300° oven for 1 hour or until done. Remove from pan and serve with Mushroom Sauce, as follows:

1 cup butter, 1 cup mushrooms, sliced, 1 cup flour, 2 cups chicken stock or broth, ¼ cup milk, ⅛ tsp. papricka, ½ tsp. chopped parsley, 1 tsp. lemon juice, salt and pepper to taste. Melt butter and add mushrooms. Simmer for 5 minutes. Add flour and blend. Gradually add stock and blend. Cook until smooth, stirring constantly. Add milk, parsley, lemon juice, salt & pepper,

Delicate Cabbage

Shred a green head of cabbage. Drop in boiling, salted, water with a dash of cayenne pepper, cover. Cook the cabbage 10 to 15 minutes in a small amount of water. Drain. Put the cabbage in a serving dish and pour melted butter over it. Serve at once. Delicate & Delicious. Not at all like ordinary cabbage!

Chicken ~ and Dumplings

-suggestions: I use a large fryer or young hen, place in a heavy pot. Almost cover with water, add an onion, sliced and 2 celery stalks. Cover and cook gently until meat is tender. Add salt to taste toward end of cooking. (Use cut-up chicken)

-and now the Dumplings ～

1½ cups flour, 2 tsps. baking powder, ½ tsp. salt, 1 heaping tbsp. shortening, 3/4 cup milk.

Sift flour, measure, add baking powder and salt, sift again. Blend in the shortening with a fork or pastry blender, add milk. Drop by tablespoonfulls onto gently boiling chicken, or stew, allowing dough to rest on meat. Cover closely and steam about 15 minutes (low flame is right). Makes 12 dumplings. If you feel you'd like lighter and more tender dumplings, add a little more milk - experiment.

Favorite Roast (easy, too!)

Take a 3 to 4 pound boneless rump roast, salt and pepper, brown on all sides in a heavy pot with a little bit of oil. Turn fire way down. Add one cup beef bouillon and four small onions. Cook 2½ to 3 hours till very tender ... What gravy!! Slice roast and serve with rice and gravy, a la Louisianne!

Cherry Fling

When I finally tried this quick, simple, easy, recipe and found how very delicious it was, well, we've served it to many guests. Always it is remarked on as something new and good. ("How _do_ you make it?")

— now for the "Fling" ~

1 can (1 lb. 5 oz.) cherry pie filling

1 pkg. Jiffy white cake mix, (or any ONE layer white mix.)

3/4 stick margarine, more or less, cut in squares

1/2 cup chopped nuts

Whip cream or Cool Whip

Heat oven to 350°. Lightly butter 8"x 8" square pan. Spread pie filling over bottom of pan. Sprinkle d_ry cake mix over cherries, pat lightly. Dot top with margarine thoroughly and cover with nuts. **Bake 45 to 50 minutes. Serve on dessert plates, cover with topping.**

<u>**Frozen Cream Cheese:**</u> 1 pt. cottage cheese (we use Schmierkäse)

1 can condensed (not evaporated) milk

1 pt. whipping cream and 1 tsp. vanilla

Work cheese through sieve. Combine cheese with condensed milk, add whipped cream and 1 tsp. vanilla. Blend and freeze.

A COBBLER is a Delicious Thing.

PEACH COBBLER

1 large size can peach halves (home style) drained.

½ tbsp. cornstarch	2 tbsps. butter
1 cup peach syrup	1 tbsp. sugar
a Pinch of nutmeg	⅓ cup light cream
1 cup Biscuit mix	Heavy cream to pass at table

Butter a 1½ qt. casserole. Place drained peach halves inside. Blend cornstarch and syrup, adding syrup a little at a time. Sprinkle in nutmeg and pour over peaches. Now — combine bisquit mix and sugar, cut in butter, then add light cream, knead until fairly smooth. Roll out ¼ inch thick on floured board to fit casserole. Place crust over peaches. Do not seal edges. Bake cobbler in a 400° oven 20 to 25 minutes until crust is golden. Serve cobbler while still warm. Pass the heavy cream - (it is tastier than whipped cream for this dish.)

The men who come to supper
will kiss the cook in appreciation.

Cheese? Slice it, grate it, melt it, toast it, blend it, no matter how you serve it there is a cheese to suit every taste, mood or occasion. (There are some 400 varieties.)

Macaroni and Cheese

grate ½ lb. sharp cheddar cheese, 2 cups, cook 8 ounces macaroni, make a medium white sauce, melting 4 tbsps. butter or margarine and blend in well 4 tbsps. flour, ½ tsp. salt, ½ tsp. dry mustard; add 2 cups milk and cook over low heat, stirring until thickened, add grated cheese, 1 tbsp. chopped onion, 1 tsp. worcestershire sauce, cooked macaroni, stirring gently until cheese is melted; then place mixture in buttered 1½ qt. casserole, top with ½ cup bread crumbs mixed with 2 tbsps. melted butter, bake 25 minutes, or until top is lightly brown in 350° oven (Not too brown)

MEAT and RICE CASSEROLE w/CHEESE

1 lb. ground, lean beef
½ cup chopped celery
½ cup chopped onion
½ cup chopped bell pepper
½ stick of oleomargarine
Cook the above for a few minutes. Do not brown. Remove from fire and add: 1 can cream of mushroom soup — 1 can chicken noodle soup — ½ cup grated sharp cheese — salt and pepper to taste — 1 tbsp. worcester sauce — 1 cup raw rice. Place in a shallow baking dish. Cover with bread crumbs. Cover, bake at 300° 1½ hours, or until rice is done.

Notes on Cheese and Fruits.

Cheese was one of the foods that came over on the Mayflower. Our standby today is cheddar cheese, mild or sharp flavor, depending on aging. Best served with tart Jonathan apples.

Swiss cheese – delicate nut-sweet flavor, best with tangy, greening, apples and green finger grapes.

Blue cheese – sharp, salty, piquant flavor. Best with sweet Anjou pears.

Gouda cheese – mild, nutty, flavor with slight tang Best with golden delicious apples.

CHEESE and DATE BREAD

¾ cup boiling water, 8 oz. dates, finely cut, 1¼ cups flour ¼ tsp. salt, 1 tsp. baking soda, ¼ cup sugar, 1 egg, 1 cup natural cheddar cheese, grated.

Pour boiling water over dates. Let stand 5 minutes. Sift flour, measure, add salt, baking soda, sugar and sift again. Add date mixture, beaten egg, and cheese to flour mixture. Mix well. Pour into a greased loaf pan. Bake in 350° oven for 50 minutes. Yield, 1 loaf bread.

—and, dear Bride

If one of your wedding gifts is an electric skillet, do use it for making pancakes—it's the greatest! Set dial at 400°, put in enough oil just to grease the bottom before adding the batch of cakes. They turn out light and perfect.

Grill cheese sandwiches in your skillet, or French fry potatoes.

Also, make a WESTERN OMELET

2 tbs. butter or oil
½ cup chopped ham
1 small onion, chopped
½ green pepper, diced

6 eggs, beaten
⅓ tsp. salt - dash of pepper
2 tbsps. catsup or chili sauce
2 tbsps. milk

Sauté ham, onion and green pepper 'till lightly brown at 330°. Reduce heat to 300°. Beat eggs, add salt, pepper, catsup and milk. Pour into pan with ham and vegetables. Keep turning up egg mixture as egg firms. When set, but still moist, turn out. 4 servings.

Also, for your skillet cooking, see page 49, "Chicken in Skillet."

Fig Preserves

These are the very best we've ever eaten: from Mrs. W. Porter Allen of Franklin, La.

Gather figs as they begin to ripen—the flavor is better. Leave some stem on (short). Wash two cups figs in very warm—not boiling—water, to which you have added some baking soda. Let stand 5 minutes. Drain well and wash in clear, cool water _twice_. Drain for 20 minutes.

Now — into a heavy, large kettle put 1½ cups white sugar and ½ cup of water. Stir well and bring to a full boil before adding figs; use medium heat.

Cook until syrup is thick and figs are medium brown in color. (Do not over cook syrup—it turns to sugar.)

When figs are cooked, let stand over night in syrup.

Next morning _heat_ but do not boil. When hot, put in standard preserve jars — 8 oz, self sealing, crystal jars are nice. See that jars are clean and scalded. When filled with figs and syrup, _seal_ each jar immediately. Place jars in hot water, boil for 5 minutes — the water _must_ cover the jars. Have on the bottom of kettle. Do not put jars touching bottom. Take jars from kettle, place upside down to cool; check seals for leakage. Never cook over 6 cups of figs and 4½ cups sugar at one time.

BROWN SUGAR CHEWS *(Olga's)*

Mix together I cup <u>dark brown sugar</u> and <u>I egg</u>. Add to this 5 rounded tbsps. <u>flour</u>, 1/4 tsp. <u>soda</u> and I cup <u>chopped nuts</u>. Then add to this mixture 1/3 stick <u>butter or oleo</u> ~ melted, not brown. Grease and flour a 8"x8" pan, pour in mixture and bake at 325° for 15 to 20 minutes. Cut in squares and roll in powdered sugar. *Use while nice and fresh.*

HOT TAMALE and BEAN DIP.   *(Chick Snowden's own.)*

I can Old El Paso hot Tamales ~ I large can Frito Bean Dip.
Mash tamales well, mix with bean dip.
Heat in double boiler. Serve hot with
Frito Chips.

Butterscotch Sauce
1½ cups light bown sugar
1/3 cup butter or oleo
3/4 cup light corn syrup
1/8 tsp. salt and I cup thin cream

Cook sugar, butter, corn syrup and salt together until sugar is completely dissolved. Add cream very slowly, stirring constantly until syrup thickens, 228°. Serve hot. Makes about 2 cups.

<u>Tips</u> from a Bride of 1947 ~ De Voe Holmes Potter, who has lived and entertained in The Hague, London, Chicago and New Orleans.

I'd say the hardest part of a meal is getting everything ready at the same time and on to that table. Two things seem to help: start very early with preparations; invite one couple at a time. Practicing "small" will give you confidence.

After you have given it your <u>all</u> relax with the thought "Here it is – take it or leave it!!"

Your goal is to have an hour to yourself before guests arrive. Be as informal as you like, but remember, using your prettiest linens and silver will give you a lot of satisfaction and candle light makes the group closer. Recovering from mistakes, such as lumpy gravy and sauces, curdled dressings, custard (not baked) that separate --- give them a short buzz in the blender and no one will be the wiser. Be sure to grate coconut, chop nuts and make cookie and cracker crumbs in the blender.

And be sure to help your husband learn to eat a balanced breakfast.

A visitor's guest book for everyone to sign becomes a cherished volume later on. And a file card box, or small loose leaf note book, in which the Bride can keep a record of : (continued next page)

(tips from a bride cont'd)

- Who comes to lunch or dinner
  When.
  What was served.
  And perhaps a note if someone doesn't like, or can't eat
       something.
—you'll find several of DeVoe's recipes in other sections.

Chick Snowden is a hostess who lives on the Bayou in an ante-bellum home, where she entertains in la garconniere. We've included two of her recipes for the bride.

If the "deep south" appeals to you, you'll be glad to know it still lives on.
     The Bayou Teche country entertains as it did over a half century ago→ beautiful homes, manners, food carefully prepared. Men in white jackets to serve. There's still an air of the handsome life under the moss draped live oak trees.

Charlene Feske's   Café Royale Punch

1 2 oz. jar instant coffee (Sanka can be used.)
2 cups boiling water
2 cups sugar
1 qt. Half and Half
1 qt. Milk
1 qt. ginger ale
1 pt. whip cream

Dissolve coffee in boiling water, add sugar, stir until dissolved. Chill in refrigerator until just before serving. In a bowl, fold in the coffee syrup, cream, milk and ginger ale. Place one tray of ice cubes in punch bowl and pour the mixture over the ice. Top with stiffly beaten whip cream, stir slightly to blend. Serves 36 punch cups.
(Cut recipe in half, or smaller, for fewer guests.)

To serve along with the punch:
Cheese straws ~ butter fingers ~
small sandwiches, nuts and cookies.

Grace at Table
("Thanks; an expression of gratitude for gifts received." Webster.)

Recently we attended a dinner given for a large group of influential people, all of them millionaires from the Carolinas, who were touring our Bayou Country. They stood in the restaurant dining room, clasped hands with their hosts, while their spokesman offered this prayer:

Come Lord Jesus our guest to be,
Bless these gifts bestowed by Thee,
Bless our dear ones everywhere.
Keep them in thy Loving Care. Amen.
(Old Moravian Blessing)

SUMMER NIGHT PUNCH
Combine, { 1 quart tea / 1 can frozen lemonade   1 pint cranberry juice / 8 ice cubes

Serve with a scoop of lemon sherbert in a glass.
With it, have: squares of mild cheese, fresh black cherries and pralines.

148

notes

ADDENDA

personal note: *The author makes no pretensions about doing* *all* *of the cooking! But the planning and preparation of certain dishes does appeal to me and I enjoy it. Also, slightly changing the seasoning of existing dishes to obtain a tastier flavor.*

Entertaining for <u>Brunch</u>. Such a good way to entertain real friends informally at an informal hour.

Let's start with <u>fruit</u> ··· Combine available fresh fruits such as strawberries, other berries in season, honey dew melon squares, cantaloupe or water-melon balls in a large bowl and pour orange juice over all and chill. OR, serve a wedge of honeydew with a section of fresh lime. OR, serve tomato juice with a fleck of curry powder and/or a dash of Tobasco sauce for masculine appeal. The <u>bread</u> can be anything from toast points to small sweet rolls, English muffins or biscuits - all <u>heated</u>. Now the pièce de résistance, <u>Rosy Baked Ham</u> (page 42), OR, <u>Curried Beef and Avocado on Toast</u> (page 41). End Brunch with an attractive tray of <u>home made</u> cookies.

Let's continue with the Brunch suggestion and not overlook the classic breakfast of bacon, browned sausage links, or ham slices, and eggs, (scrambled, creamed in patty shells, or baked.) Add grilled tomato slices - not too ripe - topped with shredded cheddar cheese and chopped chives or parsley mixed with buttered crumbs. In any case, bake the bacon or sausage links in a shallow baking pan in a 400°F. oven. Let your guests enjoy serving themselves.

recipe ::: **CANDIED APPLE RINGS** -- good surrounding a baked ham. Slice washed and cored cooking apples half inch thick. Sprinkle slices lightly with sugar. Sauté, just until tender, in a small amount of butter or oleo. Turn once during cooking. (Rosy Baked Ham, page 42.)

To broil <u>tenderloin steaks</u>, place the meat on a rack and arrange rack in broiler so that surface of meat is two to three inches below heat for inch thick steaks; three to five inches for thicker steaks. Broil until the top sides are cooked to desired degree, then season with salt, pepper and turn - using tongs to prevent piercing the meat. Now brown the other sides. Season second sides and serve, piping hot, with or without a garnish of sautéed mushrooms. Check the doneness of the meat, if you like, by making a small slit with a sharp knife near the bone and note color.

Chicken Barbecue Sauce :

The somwhat delicate flavor of chicken is easily lost in the usual barbecue sauce. We find this very good.

⅔ cup butter (oleo); 2 tbsp. sugar; 1 tsp. salt; cayenne, few grains; 2 tbsp. flour; ⅔ cup water or chicken bouillon; 2 tbsps. pickle, chopped; 2 tsps. worcester sauce; 1¼ tbsps. lemon juice; ¼ cup vinegar; ¼ tsp. Tabasco.

Melt butter and combine dry ingredients, adding to melted butter stirring until well blended. Remove from heat. Combine remaining ingredients and gradually stir into the mixture. Return to heat and cook, stirring constantly, until thick and smooth. Makes about 1⅓ cups, or enough for two broiled chickens.

For Baked Fish the following wine sauce can be used: combine ½ to 1 cup white wine, 1 finely chopped garlic clove, 2 to 3 tbsps. lemon juice, 1 bay leaf and ¼ cup melted butter or salad oil. Pour over fish in baking pan and baste occasionally.

Have you ever used liquid smoke? So helpful in barbecuing on your stove, (outside, too). Take a thick piece of smoked ham and rub with liquid smoke at least an hour before using. Place in a heavy skillet over low heat, basting from time to time, with your favorite barbeque sauce until tender and seasoned. Good with coleslaw.

Incidentally, a simple way to get a few drops of lemon juice: Pierce one end of a whole lemon with the tines of a fork and squeeze out the needed juice instead of cutting a whole lemon in half. Another hint — add a cup of crushed cornflakes to a favorite chocolate chip cookie recipe for an extra crisp cookie.

And <u>chafing dish</u> recipes; just a few.

<u>CHRISTMAS DAY BREAKFAST</u> : : Minted orange juice; (1 tbsp. finely chopped mint in one quart orange juice.)

Creamy eggs with almonds and mushrooms \ hot biscuits \ jam \ coffee.

<u>To prepare the egg dish for four to six servings:</u>

3 tbsp. butter; ¾ cup sliced mushrooms; 6 eggs, slightly beaten; 1 tsp. salt; ⅛ tsp. pepper; ½ cup coffee cream; ½ cup blanched almonds

Heat butter in chafing dish pan over direct heat; cook mushrooms until soft. Set lower pan over heat, add boiling water. Place chafing dish pan with mushrooms over this. Add eggs, salt, pepper and cream. Cook slowly, stirring until creamy. Remove from heat, sprinkle almonds over mixture and serve hot.

and for an informal supper have this menu:
Veal birds, cooked butter beans, fried rice with almonds (use cooked rice),
bananas, sprinkled with brown sugar, cooked in butter, coffee.

<u>Veal Birds</u>: 3/4 cup soft bread crumbs \ 2 tbsp. grated onion \ 1 tbsp. chopped parsley \ ½ tsp. salt and a dash of black pepper \ 3 tbsp. melted butter for stuffing \ 12 thin slices veal, lean and cut in 3 inch squares \ 2 tbsp. flour \ 1 cup meat stock (or 1 bouillon cube in 1 cup hot water).

Combine bread crumbs, onion, parsley, salt, pepper, butter and moisten stuffing with enough meat stock for proper consistency. Spread stuffing on each piece of veal; roll up and fasten with tooth picks or use thread. Dredge in flour. Heat butter in Chafing dish over direct heat, add veal rolls and brown all sides. Add beef stock; cover and cook until veal is tender. Serve two "birds" each serving: **6 servings.**

—or a <u>seafood</u> dish (plan your own menu!) <u>Oysters and Shrimp à la Louisiane.</u>
1 cup cleaned and boiled shrimp \ 1 pt. oysters \ 3 tbsp. oil \ 3 tbsp. onions, minced \ 2 tbsp. bell pepper, minced \ 1 tbsp. celery, minced \ 1 whole clove garlic, (on tooth pick for easy removal) \ 2 tomatoes, chopped \ 1 tbsp. lemon juice \ ½ tsp. salt \ ½ tsp. black pepper \ dash of thyme \ 2 tbsps. parsley, chopped.

Heat oil in Chafing dish pan over direct heat. Add onion, bell pepper, parsley, celery and garlic. Cook about 10 minutes til onion is tender, add tomato, lemon juice and seasonings, stir. Before sauce boils, add oysters and shrimp. Cook 'til oysters curl, remove garlic—serve.

154

for your personal notes and recipes

Addenda continuation, 1974

With the first complete revision of BAYOU COOK BOOK, the vast amount of time needed to hand letter new additions, rearrange the pages and re-number them, was just too much to attempt again. So an Addenda was introduced and herein we are adding some new material we trust will be found of interest.

SPOON BREAD

½ lb. butter (oleo)   1 tsp. salt
4 cups milk   3 tbsps. sugar
1 cup corn meal   6 eggs

Mix milk and butter in saucepan and bring to boil. Add corn meal, salt and sugar and stir until thick. Set aside and let cool, then add the egg yolks. Beat the egg whites until stiff and fold into the other mixture. Pour into a baking dish and bake about 45 or 50 minutes at 375° until browned. Serve at once.

(This may not be Creole, but it surely is Southern!)

SOUR CREAM BISCUITS

2 cups sifted flour
½ tsp. soda
1 tsp. salt
1½ cups sour cream (about)

Sift flour once, measure, add soda, salt, and sift again. Add enough sour cream to make soft dough. Knead lightly on floured board. Roll ½ inch thick and cut any desired shape. Bake in very hot oven (475° to 500°) 15 minutes.

BACON MUFFINS

2 cups self rising corn meal
1 to 1¼ cups milk
4 tbsps. melted shortening
2 eggs, beaten
½ cup cooked, crumbled, bacon
3 tbsps. chopped, green peppers

Put corn meal in bowl, add milk, shortening and eggs, mix well, stir in bacon and green pepper just to blend. Do not beat. Fill 12 greased muffin cups two thirds full. Bake at 450° for about 20 minutes.

DROP BISCUITS

2 cups flour   3 tsps. baking powder
2 tsps. salt – 6 tbsps. butter – 1 cup milk – ½ cup American cheese, grated

Sift the flour, baking powder and salt together. Mix with butter, milk and cheese. Knead with fingertips. Mix quickly and drop in greased skillet or muffin pan. Bake 15 minutes, hot oven, 475° to 500°.

a basic ROUX

—so, what's a ROUX? It's the basic, initial step, in a large number of Creole recipes. Many recipes list the roux ingredients, specifying the flour, shortening (cooking oil) onions, celery, bell pepper, etcetra. Some recipes simply say, "prepare a roux." Be sure to use a heavy iron skillet (sauce pan, frying pan). At a low heat, when oil is hot, add the flour. The following proportions are good to follow: 1 heaping tbsp. shortening and 1½ heaping tbsps. of flour. Continually stir until the flour is a fairly dark brown. Scorched or burnt flour ruins any roux, so watch your flame and keep stirring. Immediately add the onions etc. (chopped fine), cooking over low heat and stirring until the onions are wilted (transparent), not brown, add the liquid.   —About 2 quarts for the oil and flour mentioned above.

GUMBOS (GOMBO-from dialects of Central Africa)
A fairly basic Gumbo is on page 21. Following are Gumbo recipes from a single cook book: Chicken, Crawfish, Wild Duck and Oysters, Okra-Chicken, Crab, Oyster, Chicken-Oyster, Creole Shrimp, Catfish, Chicken-Ham, Duck, Okra-Shrimp.

Trout Marguery

3 lbs. tenderloin of trout
3 tbsps. olive oil
2 egg yokes
1 cup melted butter
20 cooked shrimp, chopped
½ cup cooked crab meat

Juice of ½ lemon
Salt and pepper and paprika to taste
½ cup sliced mushrooms
¼ cup oyster liquor
1 tsp. flour
1 tbsp. water

Place fish in pan, add olive oil and bake at 375° for 30 minutes. While fish is cooking, make hollandaise sauce. For the sauce, beat egg yolks well. Pour melted butter into yolks very slowly, stirring until it thickens. When thick add lemon juice, flour, water, salt, pepper, paprika, shrimp, crab meat, mushrooms and oyster liquor. Heat thoroughly. Place fish on platter, add oil to sauce, mix and pour over fish.

Anchovy Pecans (tasty)

Toast pecan nut meat halves in moderate oven at 350°, 5 minutes. Spread flat sufaces (bottoms) with thin layer anchovy paste. Press each two halves together. Serve immediately.

STUFFED FLOUNDER FILLETS

1 lb. spinach
  2 tbsps. fine, dry, bread crumbs
  ½ tsp. salt and ⅛ tsp. pepper
  1 tsp. prepared mustard
¼ cup finely diced onion

4 flounder fillets, about 1½ lbs
  2 tbsps. fat
  3 oz. can sliced, broiled mushrooms
  1 tsp. corn starch
2 tbsps. minced parsley ~ ¼ cup sour cream

Cook spinach, drain well, chop finely. Combine chopped spinach with bread crumbs, salt, pepper and mustard. Place a portion of spinach mixture on broad end of each fillet. Roll up and fasten with toothpick. Brush fat over rolled fillets. Arrange fish on heat-proof serving platter. Combine contents of can of mushrooms and corn starch in small saucepan. Bring to boil, stirring constantly. Pour around fish rolls. Sprinkle rolls with onion and parsley. Bake in moderate oven, 350°, until fish flakes easily, about 30 minutes. Remove from oven, top fillets with sour cream. Place fish under broiler just long enough to brown slightly, about 5 minutes. Serve immediately, makes 4 servings.

Frog Legs

Use hind legs of frog, cleaned. Put in layer on flat dish. Slice onions on top and crush 2 buds of garlic and sprinkle on top of meat. Cover with vinegar and let stand for two hours.

Drain off and boil in water to which you have added 1 tablespoon of salt and slice of lemon. Let boil for 20 minutes.

Remove from stove and drain until water has dripped off. Make a batter of:

- 1 cup flour
- 1 egg
- 1 tsp. salt
- 1/4 tsp. red pepper
- 1/2 cup milk

Dip frog legs in batter and fry in deep fat until golden brown.

-sauces & relishes for
FISH

Fried fish requires a cold sauce, such as horseradish, cucumber, remoulade, tartare or any other sharp sauce.

Boiled fish needs a tart or sour sauce, such as tartare or any other tart cream or butter sauce, such as Hollandaise.

Steamed fish requires the same sauces as for boiled fish.

Baked fish should have an onion, tomato or garlic sauce or some combination of these. Serve relishes in a plate along side of your sauce. Good ones are celery, green pepper, carrot, cabbage, sweet-sour beets, cucumber relish, hot pickled peppers, pickled onions, pickled eggs. They spark up the flavor of your fish-makes them special.

ASPIC SALAD

1 tbsp. gelatine ~ 1¾ cups canned consommé ~ 2 tsp. grated onion

Soften gelatine in ¼ cup of the cold consommé. Heat remaining consommé to boiling; add softened gelatine, stir until dissolved; add grated onion. Turn into individual molds first rinsed in cold water. Chill until firm. Unmold on lettuce on which you have placed a mound of the following: Philadelphia cream cheese, softened and mixed with 2 tbsp. finely chopped pecans or walnuts. Place 1 tbsp. of mayonnaise on the lettuce leaf. Serve with Gumbo and rice.

CREOLE WHITE BEAN
SOUP

1½ lbs. plain white beans
½ lb. lean salt pork, chopped fine
3 medium onions, chopped

1 can tomato sauce
Onion tops
Parsley ~ salt and pepper

Boil beans until tender enough to mash. Strain through colander, remove hulls. Return to pot, adding water to desired consistency. Scald salt meat. Fry, adding chopped onions and tomato sauce. Let simmer 1 hr. before adding to soup. Combine with soup and let cook together ½ hour. Before removing from heat, add chopped onion tops and parsley.

CREAMY POTATO SOUP

1 large onion, chopped
2 tbsp. butter
6 cups milk
1 tbsp. salt
1½ cups dry, instant, potato flakes

Cook chopped onion in large pan
in butter until tender. Add
milk and salt and heat just to
boiling. Remove from heat.
Stir in potato flakes. Serve
hot. Makes six cups of about
one cup each.
          Try this
I find that using Onion
and garlic powders instead
of the onion and garlic
salts, so very much better.
You get the real flavor in
seasoning.

TURNIP SOUP

4 turnips, sliced thick
1 cup ham, cubed
2 tbsps. butter
2 small onions
3 or 4 pieces celery
Salt and pepper
Water, 1 quart

Boil onions and celery until
tender. Melt butter in fry pan
and brown turnips slightly.
Add turnips to onion-celery
mixture. Brown cubed ham in
fat and add to mixture. Add
enough water to reach about
2 inches above mixture. Salt
and pepper to taste. Simmer
until turnips are melting
and breaking apart. Add
water as needed. Serves 6.

Crab Meat Soup au Bayou

1 cup crab meat — ½ lb. cheddar cheese, grated — 2 tbsps. butter —
¼ tsp. flour — 4 cups milk — Dash cayenne — 1 tbsp chives, minced
¼ tsp. salt — a few grains pepper

Melt butter and blend in flour, salt and pepper. Gradually add milk. Cook in top of double boiler, stirring constantly until thickened. Add cheese. Stir until cheese is melted. Blend in well. Add dash cayenne. Place crab meat into mixture, blending well. Simmer for a few minutes. Serves six.

French Kidney Bean Soup

3 cups kidney beans (cooked) — ⅛ tsp. pepper — 1 tsp. salt
3 tbsps. onion, minced — 2 cups tomato, canned — ¼ cup carrots, minced —
1 cup hot water

Combine beans, celery, carrots, onions, water and tomato. Bring to the boiling point and simmer gently about 40 minutes or until vegetables are tender. Stir frequently during simmering process. Press through a sieve, season and bring again to a boil. Sprinkle with parsley and grated cheese, if desired. Serves six.

VENISON STEAKS & CHOPS

Wipe meat with a damp cloth; sprinkle with salt and pepper. Brush with melted butter (oleo) or salad oil. Broil or pan fry as you would a beef steak. Rub the pan or broiler rack with garlic if desired.

∽ Doves ∽

– for every two doves use the following:
1 small can mushrooms ∽ 1 clove chopped garlic ∽ 1 tsp. chopped bell pepper ∽ 1 tsp. chopped celery ∽ 1 tbsp. chopped, crisp, bacon ∽ 1 tbsp. parsley ∽ 1 tbsp. onion tops ∽ 2 cups water ∽ 1 tbsp. flour ∽ salt, red and black pepper to taste ∽ 4 tbsp. oil ∽ 2 tbsps. sherry.

Season cleaned doves and stuff with mixture made from garlic, onions, bell pepper, celery, bacon, parsley and onion tops. Brown doves in salad oil. Remove from pot. Make a roux with 1 tbsp. flour in pot. Return doves to pot and add 1 cup water and the sherry. Cover and simmer, adding remainder of water when necessary, until doves are tender. Add mushrooms, chopped onion tops and parsley and cook 10 minutes. Serve with cooked rice. (Rice dressing, "Dirty Rice," is good, page 39.)

YAMS — *(of course we refer to sweet potatoes.)*

Since yams are so widely grown in South Louisiana, they surely must be mentioned. They are popular with meats — ham, pork, and chicken. Two combinations I hope you'll like are sliced yams with sliced apples and sausage, and, mashed yams on pineapple rings with bacon curls.

Yam Soufflé

2 cups boiled, mashed yams, 3/4 tsp. salt, 3/4 cup milk or light cream, 1/2 cup honey, 2 tbsps. cornstarch, 3 eggs, beaten, 3/4 cup pecans, corsely chopped

Blend all ingredients in order given. Place in buttered 1½ qt. casserole. Bake at 300° for 30 to 40 minutes until set. *Serves 6 to 8.*

Yams in ORANGE CUPS

1 can (No. 2½) mashed yams, 4 oranges, butter and cream, brown sugar

Cut oranges in half. Remove pulp and white membrane. Season mashed yams with soft butter, orange juice. If desired, use some of the orange pulp, cut small. Whip until fluffy. Fill orange shells and sprinkle with brown sugar. Bake at 350° until slightly glazed.

For variation, flavor mashed yams with Sherry, Cointreaux or Rum.

a good PECAN PIE

1½ cups dark molasses
1 cup sugar
4 eggs and 4 tbsps. butter
1 tsp. vanilla
1½ cups pecans, chopped
1-9 inch pie shell

In 350° oven bake pie shell 5 min.
Cook sugar and molasses 5 min.
Beat eggs and slowly add syrup.
Add butter, vanilla and nuts.
Pour into partially baked pie shell.
Cook 45 minutes at 350°. As pie
cools it will become firm.

cherries jubilee

1 No. 2 can pitted cherries, black
1 tsp. corn starch
½ cup cognac, warmed
1 qt. vanilla ice cream

Drain juice from canned cherries.
Heat ¾ cup cherry juice in a
saucepan. Make a paste of the
corn starch and 2 tbsps. of the
remaining cherry juice. Add
this to hot juice and stir until
thick and clear. Remove from
heat. Add cherries and pour
into metal pan, heatproof
casserole dish, or chaffing dish.
Ignite warm cognac and carefully pour on top of mixture.
Spoon flaming cherries over
individual servings of ice
cream. Serve immediately.
Serves 8.

Dixie Plantation ∽ EGGNOG

Enjoyed at Sarah and Monty's New Year's Eve parties.

∅ ½ gal. Eggnog ice cream   Brandy
  1 qt.   dairy Eggnog   Rum
  1 pt.   whip cream   nutmeg

∅ <u>if not available</u>, use yellow ice cream (French Vanilla).

Place the ice cream in the refrigerator section two hours before use to soften it. Place the softened ice cream in a large punch bowl, add the dairy eggnog and whip cream, mix lightly. Then add the brandy and rum to desired taste; mix by gentle stirring. The whip cream helps cut the flavor of the sweet ice cream and dairy mix. A large portion of brandy and rum helps everything and also helps the dead, sweet taste — and, does add zest to not only the eggnog but to the guests! Do not add nutmeg to the bowl but have it available.   Note: proportions of the whip cream, brandy and rum, depend upon the Hostess. So—add and sample, don't spoil the delicious eggnog taste. (Good with "nog", salted nuts, a tasty dip, finger sandwiches, small squares of fruit cake, etcetra)— and a Very Happy New Year!

-a few more notes:

Fourth edition, *Addenda* to "FOR the BRIDE", page 127.

— daughter DeVoe's <u>Lemon Mousse</u>

    1 can evaporated milk
      2 eggs
        1 cup sugar
          Juice of two lemons
            ¼ tsp. lemon extract
              1½ cups graham cracker crumbs

Chill can of evaporated milk in refrigerator over night.
Have large bowl (over 2 qt. size) chilled; also have two
small bowls. Separate eggs into small bowls. Beat egg
whites until stiff. Beat egg yokes until lemon colored,
adding 2 tbsp. lemon juice. Whip chilled milk in large
chilled bowl until frothy, gradually adding sugar. Beat in
lemon juice and extract. Beat in egg yokes. Fold in egg
whites. Pour into two 8 inch square pans which have
been spread with the crumbs, saving a small sprinkle of
crumbs to decorate the top. Freeze for 3 hours, or until
firm enough to cut. (If not needed, give one pan to a friend!)

– a pre dinner punch with a lively touch. Elegant for summer entertainment.

FRUIT PUNCH

1 can (6 oz.) frozen orange juice concentrate, undiluted, thawed; 1 can (6 oz) frozen grape fruit juice concentrate, undiluted, thawed; 2¼ cups water; ⅔ cup Apricot Nectar; 3/4 cup pineapple juice; 2 cans (12 oz. each) ginger ale, chilled; cold whole Strawberries and pineapple chunks. Mix undiluted orange and grape fruit concentrates, water, apricot nectar and pineapple juice in pitcher. Chill. Just before serving add gingerale. Make kabobs by alternating strawberries and pineapple chunks on plastic straws. Place them in tall glasses filled with ice and add the punch. Yield 2 quarts.

HOLLANDAISE SAUCE *

2 eggs thoroughly beaten; ½ stick butter, (melted); 1 lemon (juice of); 2 tbsps. water. Mix all engredients together in saucepan and place over low fire. Stir constantly. Add a pinch of salt after sauce is thoroughly heated. Stir until sauce thickens to desired consistency. Can be stored in refrigerator and reheated.

SAUCE for BAKED IDAHO POTATOES

Soften 1 8 oz package of cream cheese with ½ cup of dairy sour cream and beat until smooth and light. The mixture will give a gourmet touch to your baked potatoes.

Patty Shells

1 3oz package cream cheese, 1 stick of margarine, 1 cup all purpose flour. Have cream cheese and margarine at room temperature. Mix all ingredients together until smooth using fingers to do the mixing. Continue mixing until it balls up, then refrigerate for one hour. 'Break' the dough into 36 marble size balls, using fingers to press into small muffin pans. Bake at 425° for 10 to 12 minutes, then turn them out gently. This will make 36 patty shells.

Sautéed Crackers

A long time ago Lucie's mother, Jennie, called "Mammie" by the children in the family, fixed something to serve with coffee that became known to all of us as "Mammie's crackers." Today we accept them as a necessary accompaniment to 10 o'clock or four o'clock coffee. And they are great for a surprise quickie when friends drop in. You gently melt an extravagant amount of butter, or oleo, in a skillet. Place 8 or 10 saltine crackers flat in the skillet and sautée on both sides until they are golden-not dark—brown. Serve while real hot. (We like to use KRISPY CRACKERS by Sunshine Company.)

GREEN BEANS ALMONDINE

Mrs. Alva M. Gregg

Party French Style Green Beans

3 No. 2 cans of French Style Green Beans. (Del Monte brand.)
3/4 stick butter or margarine
1 Lemon, juice of
3/4 cups toasted Blanched, Slivered Almonds-seasoned
   salt to taste.

Heat beans 5 to 10 minutes. Drain liquid from beans. Melt butter (margarine)-do not let it brown. Add drained beans to melted butter. Next add lemon juice and seasoned salt, to your taste. Heat mixture 3 to 5 minutes. Add toasted, silvered, almonds when you are ready to serve the beans. Serves 12.

—good and easy OYSTER PIE

1 small can oysters - 2 cups milk - 2 tbsps. butter or oleo. Salt and pepper to taste (oysters are already salty). Break up 2 cups crackers atop oysters in small casserole. Add milk and butter to oysters. Bake in moderate oven until mixture turns light brown. This is a terrific dish for lunch or part of dinner.

—and a few more for the 4th edition ~ 1976. This, we trust, will be our last work on this book. Lucie, my wife, looked over my shoulder and said, "How in the world can you do this tedious work?" Without really thinking I replied, "Practice, practice; patience, patience ~ and Love." Our main interest is to provide as good an INDEX as we can, correct the few errors/omissions and include the new material. The hundreds of letter requests for this book, from all sections of this country and from Alaska and Hawaii surely shows the interest in our Creole style cooking.

Fish Piquant

2 lbs. sliced catfish
1 pt. oysters, drain, reserve liquor
½ cup cooking oil or shortening
2 tbsps. flour
1 can tomato sauce
¼ cup minced celery

½ cup minced onion
4 cloves garlic, chopped fine
1 tbsp. minced green peppers
¼ cup, minced green onions
½ cup, minced parsley
Tabaso sauce and salt to taste

Fry garlic slowly in melted shortening until dark brown (discard). On low heat, stir in flour to make roux, cook slowly, about 30 minutes until desired shade of brown is reached (not too dark). Then sauté onion, pepper, green onions, and celery until tender. Add tomato sauce, oyster liquid, and sliced fish. Simmer slowly until tender. Just before serving, add oysters. Serve with rice and garlic bread

Shrimp Stew

4 tbsp. shortening – 5 tbsp flour – ⅓ cup chopped onion – 2 cloves garlic, minced – ½ cup chopped celery – 1 8oz can tomato sauce – 3 cups water – ¼ tsp. mustard – 1 tsp. *worcester sauce – ¼ tsp. salt – ½ tsp. red pepper – 1 pound cleaned shrimp.   Heat shortening; add flour, stirring constantly until   mixture is smooth and golden brown. Add onion, garlic and celery, cook until vegetables are soft. Reduce heat and add tomato sauce, stirring carefully about 5 minutes. Add water, mustard, *worcester sauce, salt and pepper. Simmer about 20 minutes. Add shrimp; cover pan and simmer about 20 minutes. Serve in a soup bowl over cooked rice. Makes 4-6 servings. NOTE: For a more seasoned dish, when adding water, a small cheesecloth bag containing about 2 tbsp. packaged shrimp boil spices may simmer with mixture. Remove spices before serving.
*–a reminder: this contraction used in place of the longer Worcestershire.

Barbecued Smoked Chicken — Indoors –

chicken pieces, liquid B.B.Q. smoke, butter (oleo), salt and pepper
    Brush all surfaces chicken with liquid smoke. Salt and pepper and let stand 40 to 60 minutes. Place in baking dish, bake at 350°. Add melted butter (oleo) and baste with liquid smoke, turning frequently, until done to your taste.

INDEX

o denotes typical Creole recipe.

CAKES & PASTRIES

Apple Cake	56
Apricot Nectar	120
Baked Alaska	95
Buttermilk Pancakes	122
Cherry Fling	137
Chocolate Cheesecake	115
Date Torte	119
a Delicious Dessert	101
Fudge Cake	91
Georgia Strawberry Shortcake	91
Huguenot Torte	89
Lemon Sponge Cake	118
Orange Cake	118
Patty Shells	171
o Pecan Pie	166
Pecan Torte	87
Pineapple Cake	93
Pound Cake	124
Sad Cake	118
Sour Cream Cake	117

CANDY

Candied Apple Rings	150
Million Dollar Fudge	94
Nut Kisses	88
Peanut Brittle	92
o Pralines	116-123

CHEESE

Cheese	139
Cheese Biscuits	79
Cheese & Date Bread	140
Cheese & Fruits	140
Cheese Straws	80
Frozen Cream Cheese	137
Macaroni & Cheese	139
o Madame Benquet's Cheese Spread	112

COOKIES

Apricot Balls	86
Almond Crisps	121
Banana Drop Cookies	88

Brown Sugar Chews	143
Brownies	124
Butter Fingers	88
Crispy Cookies	121
Fruit Cake Cookies	85
Lemon Bars	120
Oatmeal Cookies	90
Page Boy Cookies	116
Pecan Chews	85
Whiskey Balls	86

CRABS

Baked Crab Meat	24
Boiled Crabs	23
Crab Chops	25
Crab Imperial	23
Imperial Crab	131
Seafood Gumbo	21
Shrimp-Crab Meat Casserole	16
Stuffed Crabs	24·131

CRAWFISH

Crawfish Étouffée	26
Creole Crawfish	27
Lagoon Scampi	26
Spanish Crawfish	27

DESSERTS

Baked Alaska	95
Bananas-on-the-Bayou	97
Bisquit Tortoni	119
Brandied Peaches	98
Cherries Jubilee	166
Cherry Fling	137
Cream Tarts	100
Crêpe Suzettes	103
a Delicious Dessert	101
Delicious Melba	98
Fruit Cup	99
Georgia Strawberry Shortcake	91
Irish Trifle	122
Lemon Mousse	169
Mandarin Orange Dessert	97
Peach Cobbler	138
Pecan Pie	166

178

Peaches Flambé	98
Sad Cake Ice Cream	118

DRESSINGS & STUFFINGS

Anchovy Dressing	72
Basic French Dressing	72
° "Dirty Rice"	39
Fruit French Dressing	74
Horseradish Dressing	72
Oyster Stuffing	20
Rice Dressing	39
Rouquefort Dressing	72
Vinaigrette Dressing	78

EGGS

° Cajun Cheese Casserole	68
Creamy Eggs	152
Eggs with Spinach	67
Pickled Eggs	69
° Poached Eggs, Creole	68
Scrambled Eggs, Special	68
Scrambled Eggs with Eggplant	69
Shrimp Omelet	69

Southern Fluffy Omelet	67
Western Omelet	141

FISH

Baked Fish, Wine Sauce	151
Baked Red Fish	30
° Bayou Courtbouillon	29
Broiled Fish Fillets	30
° Catfish Fortnightly	28
° Catfish Squares	133
° Fish Piquant	173
Fish Sauces & Relishes	160
Stuffed Flounder Fillets	159
Stuffed Flounder Casserole	114
Trout Almondine	28
Trout Marquery	158

FOWL

Bar B Que Smoked Chicken	174
° Breaded Fried Chicken with Creole Gravy	47
Breast of Wild Duck	53
Broiled Chicken	110

Chicken à la King	48
Chicken Avocado	50
Chicken-Bar B que Sauce	151
Chicken and Broccoli	49
Chicken Casserole	50
Chicken and Dumplings	136
Chicken Fricasee	48
o Chicken Jambalaya	55
Chicken Loaf with Mushrooms	135
Chicken Salad	72
Chicken Sandwich	50
o Chicken Sauce Piquant	51
Chicken in Skillet	49
Chicken Strata	111
o Ducks in Wine	53
o French Wild Ducks	53
Southern Chicken Pie	54
Turkey and Eggplant	52
Turkey Loaf	54
Turkey Poulette	49

FROG LEGS

Frog Legs, Fried	160

FROSTINGS & ICINGS

Cream Cheese Icing	93
Mocha Butter Frosting	92

FRUITS

Candied Apple Ring	150
Cherries Jubilee	166
French Fried Bananas	59
Fruit Cup	99
Fruit Punch	170

GAME

Doves	164
Breast of Wild Duck	52
o Ducks in Orange Wine	53
o French Wild Ducks	53
Fried Rabbit	45
Game Birds	45
o Rabbit Jambalaya	45
Squirrel	45

180

Venison Steaks & Chops ... 164

GUMBO

o Gumbos ~ 157 ✱ Roux ~ 157
o Seafood Gumbo ... 26

JELLIES & PRESERVES

o Fig Preserves ... 142
Pepper Jelly ... 43

MEATS

Baked Ham ... 42
Baked Hash ... 39
Bayou Hash ... 40
Baked Pork Chops ... 109
Beef Main Cuts ... 38
Beef and Rice with Cheese ... 37
Beef Stroganoff ... 125
Braunschweiger Glacé ... 109

o Creole Hamburger ... 36
Curried Beef ... 41
o Daube Glacé ... 35
Estouffade de Boeuf ... 113
Favorite Roast ... 136
o Grillades with Gravy ... 35
Interesting Chili Dish ... 113
o Louisiana Brisket ... 42
Louisiana Meat Loaf ... 37
Meat Balls and Noodles ... 114
Meat & Rice Casserole with Cheese ... 139
Peppered Chuck Steak ... 44
Pork Roast ... 36
Rosy Baked Ham ... 42
Sausage Balls ... 132
Sausage Royale ... 43
Sour Cream Chops ... 40
Spaghetti - Italian Style ... 61
Spanish Meat Pie ... 44
Spiced Hamburger ... 40
Tenderloin Steak ... 150

Shrimp Cocktail Sauce   14
o Shrimp Remoulade   13

SEASONINGS

Herbs and Spices   6-7-8-9-10
Onion and Garlic Powders   162
Seasoned Flour   76

SHRIMP

Barbecued Shrimp   14
o Boiled Shrimp   14
o Creole Shrimp Casserole   134
Curried Shrimp   15
Marinated Shrimp   112
Oysters and Shrimp
     à la Louisiane   153
Shrimp à la King   17
Shrimp Bisque   22
Shrimp Cocktail Sauce   14
Shrimp, Crabmeat Casserole   16

o Shrimp Creole   15
Shrimp Dip   132
o Shrimp Jambalaya   16
Shrimp Newburg   13
Shrimp Omelet   69
o Shrimp Remoulade   13
Shrimp Salad   73
Shrimp Stew   174

SOUPS

o Crab Meat Soup au Bayou   163
Creamy Potato Soup   162
o Creole White Bean Soup   161
French Kidney Bean Soup   163
o Gumbos   157
Oyster Soup   22
o Seafood Gumbo   21
Shrimp Bisque   22
Turnip Soup   162
Turtle Soup   32

TURTLE

○ Turtle Sauce Piquant   31
   Turtle Soup   32

VEGETABLES

Asparagus Casserole	59
Baked Beans	64
Barbecued Onions	60
Carrots, Green Beans & Celery	62
Cauliflower au Gratin	63
Chopped Spinach	57
Cooking Artichokes	59
Corn Sauté with Peppers	58
○ Creole Okra	62
Delicate Cabbage	135
Eggs with Spinach	67
French Fried Asparagus	57
○ Fried Okra	61
Green Beans with Cheese	64
○ Pickled Okra	112
Quick, Tasty, Sandwich	134
○ Red Bean and Rice	57
Scrambled Eggs with Eggplant	69
Green Beans Almondine	172
Stuffed Artichokes	77
○ Stuffed Eggplant	65
Sweet Potatoes and Orange	58
Tomato-Eggplant Casserole	60
Turkey & Eggplant de España	52
Yams	165
Yams à la Haiti	123
Yams in Orange Cups	165
Yam Soufflé	165

THE PERFECT GIFT

Let this unique, hand lettered BAYOU COOK BOOK
solve your Gift problems. For the bride, the
experienced hostess, birthdays, showers
anniversaries & and, keep in mind,
it's an excellent "Gentleman's Companion."

—and now, turn back to page 56.
Read again "A Good Basic Recipe."
(—and follow, follow, follow.)

au Revoir.

For additional copies of Bayou Cook Book
write: Pelican Publishing Company
1101 Monroe Street
Gretna, Louisiana 70053